The NCTE High School Literature Series

The NCTE High School Literature Series offers classroom teachers in-depth studies of individual writers. Grounded in theory, each volume focuses on a single author and features excerpts from the writer's works, biographical information, and samples of professional literary criticism. Rich in opportunities for classroom discussion and writing assignments that teachers can adapt to their own literature curriculum, each book also offers many examples of student writing.

Volumes in the Series

Nikki Giovanni in the Classroom: "The same ol danger but a brand new pleasure" (1999), Carol Jago

Alice Walker in the Classroom: "Living by the Word" (2000), Carol Jago

Sandra Cisneros in the Classroom: "Do not forget to reach" (2002), Carol Jago

Raymond Carver in the Classroom

■ ■

"A Small, Good Thing"

The NCTE High School Literature Series

Susanne Rubenstein

Wachusett Regional High School

NATIONAL COUNCIL OF TEACHERS OF ENGLISH
1111 W. KENYON ROAD, URBANA, ILLINOIS 61801-1096

Staff Editor: Bonny Graham
Interior Design: Jenny Jensen Greenleaf
Cover Design: Jenny Jensen Greenleaf and Tom Jaczak

NCTE Stock Number: 38314
ISSN 1525-5786

Library of Congress Cataloging-in-Publication Data
Rubenstein, Susanne, 1954–
    Raymond Carver in the classroom : "a small, good thing" / Susanne Rubenstein.
        p. cm. — (The NCTE high school literature series, ISSN 1525-5786)
    Includes bibliographical references.
    ISBN 0-8141-3831-4
    1. Carver, Raymond—Study and teaching (Secondary) 2. Carver, Raymond—Criticism and interpretation I. Title. II. Series.
    PS3553.A7894z857 2005
    813' .54—dc22

                                      2005008474

If we're lucky, writer and reader alike, we'll finish the last line or two of a short story and then just sit for a minute, quietly. Ideally, we'll ponder what we've just written or read; maybe our hearts or our intellects will have been moved off the peg just a little from where they were before. Our body temperature will have gone up, or down, by a degree. Then, breathing evenly and steadily once more, we'll collect ourselves, writers and readers alike, get up, "created of warm blood and nerves" as a Chekhov character puts it, and go on to the next thing: Life. Always life.

−Raymond Carver, "On *Where I'm Calling From*"

Contents

■ ■

Acknowledgments

This book exists because many great, good people did many "small (and not so small), good things" to aid me in the writing. To all of them, I am very grateful. First, I thank Kurt Austin at NCTE who had confidence in me and in my passion for Raymond Carver. I thank my friends and colleagues, people like Lynn, Cathy, and Deb, with whom I can share my love of Carver and lively conversation about his work. I thank my students who trust me enough to take a chance on Carver's writing and who later carry him from my classroom in their hearts. I thank Jp for his technical support and Skip for his patience with my work on this project. And if I could, I'd thank Carver himself because when I teach his words within the walls of Room 224, I, like the narrator of "Cathedral," don't "feel like [I'm] inside anything." And that's when teaching is pure joy.

Introduction

■ ■

They call him Ray. Ray, as in "Are we going to read more Ray today?"
or "D'ya think Ray would've liked my story?" For my students,
Raymond Carver is as real as their baseball coach, the lunch line
lady, or the man who drives the bus in the morning. I don't dissuade
them. I think "Ray" would have welcomed their friendship.

When I first started teaching the writing of Raymond Carver in
the 1980s, I was a fairly new teacher with a very new course called
New Literature. A colleague and I developed the course, believing
that there was an entire body of literature out there—good *new* literature—that high school students rarely encountered. We believed
that once introduced to this literature, students might develop a life-
long love of it and so carry away from the course something far greater
than a grade. In those days, we called this writing "*New Yorker* fiction," and we bought class subscriptions to the magazine and dove
into new stories every week, sometimes floundering right along with
our students as we attempted to make meaning of the work. As time
went on, we honed our curriculum and identified the authors that
students needed to know, particularly those writers of the 1970s and
1980s who introduced minimalism to reading audiences and changed
the shape of American fiction. Yet even as we read and reacted, dis-
cussed and debated, argued and ultimately altered our reading lists
and assignments, one name stood fast: Raymond Carver. Each se-
mester we opened the course with Carver's fiction, and we caught

our students, students of all academic levels who had never read anyone like Raymond Carver but who became ardent fans, begging to borrow his collections—*Will You Please be Quiet, Please?*, *What We Talk About When We Talk About Love*, and *Cathedral*—stacked on the desk.

Twenty-some years have passed and New Literature has continued to change. Some days I wonder if it should even be called New Literature any more, since the writers of the seventies are certainly not new these days. And of course, as the body of very contemporary literature grows and the works of brand-new writers pepper the pages of magazines and anthologies, it becomes even more of a challenge to fit in all the writers I want to teach, and some semesters one gets short shrift while another takes center stage. But not Ray. Carver always gets the spotlight. He opens the curtain on the course, and after that first act, my students leave applauding, the one problem being that they aren't too eager to let anyone else perform. So each year I found myself adding just a little more Carver—a new story, a few more poems, another connection with art or literature—until suddenly I realized that Carver didn't have to stay put in New Literature. He now comes to Contemporary American Culture, and he's been visiting my Creative Writing class. Certainly he would be just as much at home in an American literature survey course, in a twentieth-century writers course, or in a short fiction class, and any grade 10, 11, or 12 English curriculum would definitely be strengthened with the addition of Carver's fiction, poetry, and essays.

Why do students like Carver's work so much and what do they learn from it? I hope this book will answer those questions, but perhaps a line from one of my students' pieces explains the attraction best. In a "review" of Carver's fiction cleverly titled "Everybody Loves Raymond . . . Carver!" Casey writes, "Carver is one of those writers who says what he means and means what he says." Although the critics may say it in a more scholarly fashion, the idea is the same. Carver, like the other minimalist writers whom he, in a sense, "fathered," tells it like it is—even if it isn't pretty. He can write honestly of lives that are down and out, because for many years he lived such a life. Carver's fiction and poetry speak for a blue-collar class who really had no voice in contemporary American literature before Carver gave them one. He says, "'But this is my world. . . . I'm a full-time member of the working poor. I was one as a child, and I've been one as an adult'" (Riotta 249). His writing describes the pain of poverty, the dangers of alcohol, and the struggles of people—friends, lovers, parents, children, even strangers—trying to forge relationships in a world where even simple survival seems too difficult. Yet somehow in the midst of all this sadness, all this "down-and-out-ness," there is always what a student once inventively referred to as a "ray" of hope: that innate human desire to be better than we are, to make something good of our lives. Beyond all the literary learning my students get from reading Raymond Carver, that is, I believe, the most important thing they take away from his words. His writing teaches them to believe in themselves and to understand that they can shape their futures, whatever the obstacles they face. I will never forget the student, a senior who found his life moving in a downward spiral, who turned to me and said, "My life's going like Carver's—and I don't know how to stop it." Then he paused and gave a brave Carver-like shrug. "But he changed. So maybe I can too."

In a 1984 interview in the *New York Times Magazine*, Carver said, "If I write a story and somebody connects up with it in some way, is moved by it and reminded of his humanness, then I'm happy. What more can I want?" (Weber 95). As a teacher, I would change only one word in those lines: "If I *teach* a story and somebody connects up with it in some way, is moved by it and reminded of his humanness, then I'm happy. What more can I want?" Teaching Raymond

Carver's work makes me this kind of happy, and I'm convinced that any teacher who brings him into the classroom will experience that same exhilaration.

1 Where Life and Art Intersect

■ ■

I was in Spain the summer Raymond Carver died, August 1988. I remember hearing a snippet of conversation in a café in the city of Seville. My ear caught the English traveling out from behind a newspaper at the next table: "Raymond Carver . . . died . . . lung cancer." I felt a quick pang of sorrow. A writer whose work I had come to love was gone. Now, somehow, in the years since Carver's death, my feeling of loss grows greater. At age fifty, Carver was at his prime as a writer. His fiction was becoming more expansive, and his poetry was flowing from him in a way it never had before. Ironically, only a very short time before the diagnosis was made of the cancer that would kill him, Carver spoke of the joy he had found recently in his writing: "I've never had a period in my life that remotely resembles that time. I mean, I felt like it would have been all right, you know, simply to have died after those sixty-five days. I felt on *fire*" (Schumacher 218).

Raymond Carver has been called the father of minimalism, a pioneer of "dirty realism," and the voice of "blue-collar despair" (Weber 84). His writing is taut and tense and on-the-surface simple, and yet his short, stripped-down stories and poems say so much more than they seem to at first glance. He is a writer who changed the style of American fiction and who, in the 1970s, had an influence on a generation of writers much like that of Hemingway in the 1920s. Because of his absolute honesty, Carver makes his readers feel the sense of alienation that is such a part of contemporary life—and yet somehow still believe in the human spirit.

I could begin teaching Raymond Carver by telling my students these things. I could introduce them to Carver with a lecture on minimalism, offer them a raft of critical reviews, or trace the development of his work in the pattern of his life. But I don't. I start instead by giving them one Carver story, maybe the one about the baby being pulled apart, or the one about the blind man who teaches a sighted man to see, or maybe even the one that ends with the ominous words, "'It has to do with Scotty, yes'" ("The Bath" 56). All I know is that I only have to give my students one Carver story and they ask for more. They want to stay in what has come to be known as Carver Country, "a place we all recognize. It's a place that Carver himself comes from, the country of arduous life" (Weber 88).

In a 1983 interview for the *Paris Review*, Carver said, "you have to know what you're doing when you turn your life stories into fiction" (Simpson and Buzbee 41). Despite the strong autobiographical feel to Carver's work, he was adamant that the facts of life could not simply be translated into the fabric of fiction.

> You're told time and time again when you're young to write about what you know, and what do you know better than your own secrets? But unless you're a special kind of writer, and a very talented one, it's dangerous to try and write volume after volume on The Story of My Life. . . . A little autobiography and a lot of imagination are best. (41)

But it's not quite that clear-cut, for there is a paradox in Carver's work, a paradox he sums up well when he writes, "Most of what I write is about myself, even though I never write anything autobiographical" (Tromp 79).

This is a concept we need to communicate when we ask students to write about what they know. Blame it on a lack of reading at an early age or a typical childhood spent more on video games and television than in imaginary play, but whatever the reason, students today seem less able to invent, to use their minds in a creative fashion, than students twenty years ago. When I ask my students to write stories, too many of their pieces are such strictly factual memoirs that they lack the spark that makes a story sing. Often the "original" plot lines mimic those of the action adventures or soap operas adolescents watch on the TV or movie screen. Yet as we study Carver's life, students begin to see that while Carver's art does draw closely on his life, it's not bound by it, and it gains intensity through the invented material. My students come to recognize that Carver is a man who knows from living, breathing experience of what he writes, but he has the creative vision to give his life stories a new life, and, in doing so, he gives them extraordinary power.

> Writers can't write strict autobiography—it would be the dullest book in the world. But you pull something from here, and you pull something from over here, well it's like a snowball coming down a hill, it gathers up everything that's in its way—things we've heard, things we've witnessed, things we've experienced. And you stick bits and pieces here and then make some kind of coherent whole out of it. (Carver qtd. in Sexton 132)

Although Carver contends that "[n]one of my stories really *happened*, of course" (Simpson and Buzbee 40), what gives his fiction such heart is that each and every story could have happened, and in just the way he tells it. Carver captures the voice and view of the lower class. His characters have been described as "ordinary people rescued from the bin of anonymity" (Caldwell

244). Often he allows them a moment of epiphany, sometimes one of pure grace. He sets many of his stories in the Pacific Northwest, a place he knew well and loved deeply. And then he tells the truth. This is why my students love Carver, because his fiction speaks the truth, because the people who fill his pages and the problems they face are real, though sometimes we wish they weren't.

It's this kind of heartfelt reaction to Carver's life and work that can be used so effectively to inspire good writing in the high school classroom. As we study Carver's biography and make connections between Carver's life and his fiction and poetry, I set my students to writing their own stories, stories like Carver's snowballs, with a hard, cold core of truth, stories that "roll along," growing larger and greater with the inventions, distortions, and just plain lies that are the stuff of fiction. As we do draft work, I ask students to make a list of these "fabrications," and in response groups they work to develop those ideas that give the story life. At the center of each story, though, is something that does bear witness to reality, and in the final drafts they hand in, I ask my students to boldface that line—that one true thing—that inspired the story. Perhaps it's a person, a remembered line of dialogue, or a sudden realization. I've read lines like "His mother made him go to camp that summer," and "If only he'd kissed me before he drove away." Whatever the line of truth is, it's enough to get them started as storytellers, and it makes them appreciate how Carver and so many other writers use pieces of their pasts to invent a new world in the present.

The Early Years

The past for Carver began in Clatskanie, Oregon. Raymond Clevie Carver Jr. was born on May 25, 1938, to Clevie Raymond Carver and Ella Beatrice Casey. In 1941 he and his family moved to Yakima, Washington, where his father worked in a sawmill. Much has been written about Carver's difficult childhood, one that was affected by poverty and his father's alcoholism. Yet Carver himself speaks of his childhood as "fairly conventional in many respects" (McCaffery and Gregory 80) and talks of his father's storytelling, especially about hunting and fishing, as a positive influence, one that helped to turn Carver into what he calls

> [a] dreamy kid. I wanted to be a writer and I mostly followed my nose as far as reading was concerned. I'd go to the library and check out books on the Spanish conquistadors, or historical novels, whatever struck my fancy. . . . Mainly I just wanted to hunt and fish and ride around in cars with other guys. Date girls. . . . But I did want to write, which might have been the only thing that set me apart from my friends. (80)

My students love this stuff, the image of a writer as a kid who can love "[h]unting late into that golden afternoon / for grouse. Following deer paths, / pushing through undergrowth" ("Wenas Ridge" 75) and writing equally. "Wenas Ridge," the story of "[t]hree of us that fall. Young hoodlums—" (75), is one of my favorite poems to read with students, and it can be used to inspire them to write about an actual place where their own lives took a turn. In prose or poetry, they try to capture the physical landscape as well as the significant moment. This is what Greg does in his piece about a midnight foray onto a golf course:

> The dark carpet of green rolled out in front of us. The sky was clear, lit by moon and stars. The warm air of the summer night sat on my shoulder, and the taste of the moist layer of silky dew on the fresh cut grass sat on my tongue as I inhaled deeply. The night sky, the grass, the moon, and the trees that swayed

in the wind all gave me a feeling of nature's freedom. A burst of
emotion and tension shot out of me.

—*Greg Jonaitis*

In Carver's poem, the appearance of a snake leads him to a
metaphor, one that reflects another segment of Carver's life: "I
married the girl I loved, yet poisoned her life. / Lies began to coil
in my heart and call it home" ("Wenas Ridge" 76). Though, with
Carver's admonition about autobiography versus fiction in mind,
I caution students not to take his words as the precise truth of his
life, the connection here is more than coincidental.

At nineteen Carver married his sixteen-year-old girlfriend
Maryann Burk. Within two years, the couple had two children,
Christine and Vance. This was a difficult period for Carver and
his wife. Although Carver dreamed of being a writer, the responsibilities of fatherhood demanded that he take a series of low-
level and low-paying jobs instead, working as a custodian, a
delivery boy, a service station attendant, and a mill worker
(McInerney 24). A move to Paradise, California, in 1958, however, brought a stroke of good luck to Carver when he enrolled in
a creative writing course taught by John Gardner at Chico State
College. Despite the fact that he and his wife were, as Carver
termed it, "stone broke" ("John Gardner" 107), Carver recognized
the importance of education: "Understand that nobody in my family had ever gone to college or for that matter had got beyond the
mandatory eighth grade in high school. I didn't *know anything*,
but I knew I didn't know anything" (107). When we read these
lines, I can almost see the proverbial light go on in some of my
students' heads. Carver's essay reminds them that anything is
possible, that they can look beyond the life that seems laid out for
them, and that with hard work, hope, and some luck, anything is
possible.

The Writing Life

For Carver, luck was this chance connection with John Gardner. Gardner was then an unpublished writer, but it was he who introduced Carver to a literary world and a literary process that would influence Carver for the rest of his life. Gardner demanded that his small band of students read Hemingway, Faulkner, Porter, and Chekhov, the last becoming one of Carver's primary influences. He made them familiar with the "little literary magazines," giving Carver his first introduction to a world of *"living authors"* ("John Gardner" 111). And he taught them the value of reader response and revision. Carver writes of how closely Gardner read his students' work: "We'd discuss commas in my story as if nothing else in the world mattered more at that moment—and, indeed, it did not" (112). Gardner was never hesitant to point out problems and suggest revisions, but "[h]e was always looking to find something to praise" (112), and Carver adds, "Seeing these comments, my heart would lift" (112). These are things I tell my students when they work in response groups—and things I remind myself when even one more paper to grade seems too much!

Despite Gardner's inspiration and the passion Carver had for writing, the 1960s were stressful years as Carver, only in his twenties, tried to be husband, father, student, worker, and writer. In 1960 he moved his young family to Eureka, California, in search of work. He transferred to Humboldt State College and within three years earned his BA. He was beginning to publish in small literary magazines but had yet to find the voice that would mark him. In the fall of 1963, with the aid of a small fellowship, he was given the opportunity to study at the Iowa Writers' Workshop, where he experimented with various styles and voices. Throughout the midsixties, he continued to work blue-collar jobs, and he continued to write.

The year 1967 marked a turning point for Carver, one of both highs and lows. It was the year of his father's death, the year the Carvers filed for bankruptcy, and the year he published "Will You Please Be Quiet, Please?," a story that was included in *The Best American Short Stories 1967*. It was also the year he was hired as a textbook editor at Science Research Associates (SRA) in Palo Alto, California, his first white-collar job and one that lasted almost three years, providing more stability for the Carver family.

When his job at SRA was terminated in 1970, Carver, backed by severance pay and a National Endowment for the Arts Discovery Award, made the decision to write full time. In June 1971, his short story "Neighbors" appeared in *Esquire* magazine. This success was due in part to the support of another important, albeit controversial, mentor, Gordon Lish, who was then fiction editor at *Esquire*. Lish had read earlier submissions from Carver—and had rejected them—but he encouraged Carver to continue to send him work. When "Neighbors" was accepted for publication, it seemed Carver had "made it." But nothing in Carver's world was ever so easy.

> In one regard, things had never seemed better. But my kids were in full cry then . . . and they were eating me alive. My life soon took another veering, a sharp turn, and then it came to a dead stop off on a siding. I couldn't go anywhere, couldn't back up or go forward. It was during this period that Lish collected some of my stories and gave them to McGraw-Hill, who published them. For the time being I was still off on the siding, unable to move in any direction. If there'd once been a fire, it'd gone out. ("Fires" 105–6)

It may have been alcohol that doused that fire. Carver had begun drinking steadily. The stress of a tempestuous marriage, the pressures of an artist's life, and a genetic inheritance combined to make Carver easy prey to alcohol. In one of his most moving poems, "Photograph of My Father in His Twenty-Second Year," he writes, "Father, I love you, / yet how can I say thank you, I who can't hold my liquor either, / and don't even know the places to fish?" ("Photograph of My Father" 7).

This Carver poem is often used as a model when teachers ask students to write from photographs, and any student who hasn't had that experience would benefit from such an assignment. In addition, *To Write and Keep Kind* (Walkinshaw), an excellent 1992 documentary of Carver's life, includes moving material on Carver's relationship with his father that serves as a backdrop for this poem.

Carver takes this voice and this family problem further in another poem, "To My Daughter," reflecting on the sad legacy carried in the Carver family by alcohol. The poem is brutally frank and wrenching as the poet begs his daughter to stop her drinking, in hopes that she can escape the physical and emotional devastation he knows it brings. It ends with the lines "Daughter, you can't drink. / It will kill you. Like it did your mother, and me / Like it did" (71). These are lines that stop many of my students cold, and they hear, in the desperate voice of the poet-father, echoes of somber advice they have been given—or perhaps that they themselves have given to others. I call this a "LISTEN To Me" poem, and I ask them to write one of their own, a poem in which the poet speaks to a particular reader as indicated by the title "To _____." Though students often choose to use their own voice as that of the speaker and to be the giver of advice, it's always interesting to me (and, I suspect, enlightening to them) to read the poems of students who try to capture the voice—and viewpoint— of someone in their own lives, a parent, a teacher, even an older sibling, who has something wise and weighty to say to them. Always there's a student who asks, "Does this have to be true?," and always I remind them of Carver's conviction that writers, though they bear witness to something that has really happened, still make that truth their own.

To the Lax Sophomore

Every day after school you come home
And say you're going to work harder
But as soon as no one is watching
You turn on the TV
Escape to your dream world
Why do you procrastinate?
Why do you push yourself
Till 1 in the morning finishing the essay?
School is a battlefield, kid,
And this war is nowhere near over
But you just sit around
While you wait for something big to happen
To distract you
You coast and try to hold out till the end
But the grades don't coast
They plummet along with your ambitions
Of doing well this year.

—*Nathaniel Blake*

For Carver, the content of "To My Daughter" was sadly all too true. Alcohol was the "poison / to [his] family" (70) and one of the primary reasons for the destruction of Carver's marriage. Despite his literary successes in the early seventies—a Wallace E. Stegner Fellowship at Stanford University, a series of visiting lecturer positions, and continued publication, including his first major-press short story collection, *Will You Please Be Quiet, Please?*, in 1976—Carver's life was in turmoil and alcohol was at its roots. The drinking was interfering with his teaching and hindering his writing. He often lived apart from his family, and when he and Maryann were together, they fought fiercely. Most significant, alcohol was seriously damaging Carver's health. He was hospitalized repeatedly, and the doctors spoke of "wet brain" and life-threatening liver damage.

Then in 1977, with the help of Alcoholics Anonymous, Carver stopped drinking: "I had my last drink on June 2, 1977. I'm more proud of that than of any other accomplishment in my life" (Tromp 77).

But sobriety did not bring immediate happiness or career success. For Carver it was a continued struggle to ameliorate the stormy relationships he had with his wife and children and to find his voice and his way as a writer without the support of alcohol. That effort was aided by an introduction that same year to the poet and fiction writer Tess Gallagher, the woman who would become a partner in all aspects of his life. In Carver's words, "And then there's Tess. My life changed dramatically the day I met her" (Kellerman 40).

The Good Years

Gallagher is considered to be one of the most important influences on Raymond Carver, in terms of both his private and his public life. By July 1978, Carver's turbulent marriage to Maryann had ended (the divorce was made legal in 1982), and Carver began to pursue a relationship with Gallagher. The two began living together in 1979, their varied residences from Texas to Washington to Arizona to New York determined by the teaching positions each held. For the next nine years, the remaining years of Carver's life, the two were partners, as lovers, friends, colleagues, and collaborators, and as writers who strengthened each other's work through their honesty and their passion for art: "Gallagher is a 'very tough' critic, Carver says. 'She cuts me no slack at all, and that's the best way'" (Moffet 242).

The early eighties were good years for Carver. He published *What We Talk About When We Talk About Love* in 1981, a collection that garnered excellent reviews and was regarded as the prototype for the new minimalist school of fiction (see Chapter 2), although Carver much preferred to call himself a "precisionist" (*Carver Country* 18). This collection has also become the centerpiece of a controversy involving Carver's work. The stories in *What We Talk About When We Talk About Love* are among some of the most stripped down of any published Carver stories. They're short, many with unresolved endings; the language and sentence structure are simple and unadorned; and there's a strong nihilistic tone to the work. Some Carver scholars maintain that this extreme minimalist style reflects Carver's view and vision at the point in his life in which these stories were written. Others contend that despite the positive reception the volume received, Carver was unhappy with many of the stories in the book because of the editing done to them by his editor Gordon Lish. They argue that the style of the stories results more from the editing work of Lish than from the revision work of Carver. Whatever the truth (and it's unlikely to ever be fully determined), Carver did ultimately either revise or "unedit and revive" certain stories from *What We Talk About When We Talk About Love*, and many were republished in the 1988 collection *Where I'm Calling From*. The changes in these stories provide an excellent lesson for students on the power of revision (see Chapter 3), and they can spark good classroom conversation on the issue of author ownership.

Whatever the level of discord between Carver and Lish, it definitely did exist, as evidenced by a fervent letter Carver wrote to Lish as he completed the manuscript of *Cathedral* in 1982. In the letter, Carver pleads to maintain control of his own words: "I can't undergo [that] kind of surgical amputation and transplantation. . . . Please help me with this book as a good editor, the best . . . not as my ghost" (Max 40).

Cathedral, named for its most well-known story and one of Carver's best, was published in 1983 as Carver wanted it, for the most part. The collection received rave reviews and earned Carver nominations for a National Book Critics Circle Award in 1983 and a Pulitzer Prize in 1984. *Fires: Essays, Poems, Stories* was also published in 1983, and in that same year Carver was awarded a Mildred and Harold Strauss Livings Award, a five-year fellowship from the American Academy and Institute of Arts and Letters that allowed him to give up teaching. Now virtually free from financial worries, Carver instead faced the pressures of fame and so retreated to Sky House, Gallagher's home in Port Angeles, Washington, where he could write relatively undisturbed.

At this point, Carver turned to poetry with a new zeal. Although poetry, for a number of years, had taken a backseat to his fiction, in the mideighties Carver found new inspiration. He was very productive, publishing poems in *Poetry* magazine and in his own collections *Where Water Comes Together with Other Water* (1985) and *Ultramarine* (1986). The publication of his poetry showed readers another side of Carver, a side just as honest as that evidenced in his fiction but somehow more intimate and vulnerable. Although he's generally known as a fiction writer, for Carver poetry had always been "very close to my heart" (Applefield 211), so close in fact that in June 1987 he said, "So I suppose on my tombstone I'd be very pleased if they'd put 'poet and short-story writer—and occasional essayist.' In that order" (Boddy 197). The line has a tragic irony to it. Only a few months later Carver was diagnosed with cancer. So too does his last piece of published fiction eerily presage his death. "Errand" was published in the June 1, 1987, *New Yorker*, the story inspired by a new biography, *Chekhov* by Henri Troyat ("On 'Errand'" 197). Carver had always deeply admired Chekhov's work, and, in the course of reading this biography, he became particularly gripped by a description of the night of Chekhov's death, July 2, 1904 (197). The scene involved the ordering of champagne by Chekhov's doctor as Chekhov lay dying: "But this little piece of human business struck me as an extraordinary action. Before I really knew what I was going to do with it, or how I was going to proceed, I felt I had been launched into a story of my own then and there" (197). The story is an excellent example of how researched reality and imaginative invention can be blended into the perfect tale. It re-creates the moment Chekhov first hemorrhaged from the tuberculosis that killed him and traces his decline to the final ordering of champagne at his deathbed, an ending Carver struggled with and ultimately sought Gallagher's help in bringing to resolution (Max 51). "Errand," though "a good deal different from anything I'd ever done before" ("On 'Errand'" 198), is considered one of Carver's finest stories. The power of the story is magnified by the fact that only weeks after its publication, Carver himself was diagnosed with lung cancer.

Carver, a man who smoked sixty cigarettes a day (Caldwell 243), quit smoking cold turkey. In October 1987, he underwent surgery to remove much of his left lung. In March 1988, he completed a series of radiation treatments, but the cancer reappeared.

Despite the clearly ominous course the disease was taking, Carver was buoyed by the May publication of *Where I'm Calling From* and by his induction into the American Academy and Institute of Arts and Letters. And on June 17, aware that time was running out, he and Gallagher married in Reno. On the morning of August 2, 1988, Carver died at home in Port Angeles, Washington.

Raymond Carver's life was one of extremes. The early years were grim, bleak, and difficult as he battled poverty, alcohol, and relationships gone wrong: "Life / was a stone, grinding and sharpening" ("The Autopsy Room" 150). His last years were good ones, bright with career success and personal happiness: "Alive, sober, working, loving and / being loved by a good woman" ("Gravy" 118). I know there are those who might argue that the hard facts of Carver's life are not the sort of stuff adolescents ought to grapple with. My students and I would disagree. My students seem to draw strength from Carver. Somehow his life embodies for them something of the American Dream. He reminds them that you don't have to start with anything but a dream, a passion, something that sets you on fire. Add to that persistence and drive and heart—and there is hope. When in a poem he tells them what you need for painting, they understand that this is exactly what you need for living too: "Indifference to everything except your canvas. / The ability to work like a locomotive. / An iron will" ("What You Need for Painting" 142).

Raymond Carver found through his passion for writing the sort of success that allowed him to face even an early death with equanimity and something akin to joy. We hear this in his poem "Gravy": "'Don't weep for me,' / he said to his friends. 'I'm a lucky man / I've had ten years longer than I or anyone / expected. Pure gravy'" ("Gravy" 118). Each year as we read these last lines, there is silence in my classroom. My students don't always understand the colloquial meaning of the term *gravy*, but they do understand both the tragedy and the beauty inherent in those lines. They understand Carver Country.

2 Writing from Models

■ ■

Today the Carver story I hand my students is two pages long. It's aptly named "Little Things," and it's met with enthusiasm, because what high school student can complain about a reading assignment of that length? I tell them we'll read the story together right now, and so we're plunged into the middle of an argument, an argument between a he and a she in a little kitchen. Clothes are thrown into a suitcase, furious words are exchanged, and suddenly a baby starts crying. And then he's pulling on one arm of the baby and she's pulling on the other, and "[i]n this manner, the issue was decided" ("Little Things" 154).

Now my students are wishing for another page.

"In *what* manner?" one calls.

"What happened?" asks another. "Who got the baby?"

"Is the baby OK?" questions a third.

And ultimately they all want to know who these people are and what they're fighting about anyway.

I love minimalist fiction. I love how, precisely because it seems so slim and slight, it compels readers to become deeply involved. In order to fill in the gaps, readers must bring to the story their own experience. They become participants in the world the writer has created, a world, they realize, that is often very much like their own.

"I think I know these people," says Dave, smirking.

"Yeah. I babysit for them!" calls Lisa, and there's laughter, but it's just a bit rueful.

"He's leaving because she cheated on him," announces Ryan.

"No way. He cheated on her!" This from a contingent of girls in the third row.

"No," says Katie thoughtfully. "I think he lost his job. I think they're both just stressed out." She's studying the text, the very few lines of description that open the story and that express a mood of dreary desperation. "'Cars slushed by on the street outside, where it was getting dark,'" she reads. "'But it was getting dark on the inside too'" (152).

We're barely ten minutes into the period, and I already know we could go on forever. Carver has caught these students. They've become fans of minimalism.

I always offer up silent apologies to Carver at this point. Despite his literary reputation as the father of minimalism, he did not like to be called a minimalist writer. In a 1983 interview for the *Paris Review*, he spoke of a reviewer who called him a minimalist writer: "The reviewer meant it as a compliment. But I didn't like it. There's something about 'minimalist' that smacks of smallness of vision and execution that I don't like" (Simpson and Buzbee 44). But despite his personal rejection of the term, Carver is widely seen as the writer who introduced the minimalist style to American fiction in the 1970s. In doing so, he, like Hemingway decades before, influenced an entire generation of young writers—a group of whom, Jay McInerney among them, became known as the literary Brat Pack. Their very contemporary and very minimalist stories filled the pages of the best magazines and journals in the United States in the early 1980s—and so began a renaissance of the short story.

The Tip of the Iceberg

There are obviously strong parallels between the work of Carver and Hemingway. Carver greatly admired Hemingway's writing and saw it as an influence on his own work. He called "Cat in the Rain" "one of my favorite stories by Ernest Hemingway" (Pope and McElhinny 17), so I like to offer my students this story as we begin reading Carver and other early minimalists in order to remind them that literature develops from the writing that comes before it. As a companion piece to "Little Things," "Cat in the Rain" works particularly well because it too captures a moment of tension between a couple. On the surface, Hemingway's young American wife and her husband George seem far less downtrodden and desperate than Carver's people. They are guests at an Italian hotel, spending a dismal morning bickering, on one level, over a cat that has been left out in the rain. Though they are more circumspect in their language than the he and she of "Little Things," the reader feels their marriage unraveling and knows that the wife's desire to bring the cat inside represents more than a compassionate urge to rescue a damp feline. The setting of rain and darkness, the conflict between the two characters, the emphasis on dialogue, and the stripped-down language all offer a sharp parallel to "Little Things," and so the two stories taken together provide a perfect vehicle to discuss connections in literature. Students realize that while Carver, through his writing and his teaching, did bring the minimalist style to a new generation of readers and writers, this style was not entirely innovative.

In particular I like to talk about the fact that Carver's writing demonstrates the same "iceberg structure" for which Hemingway is known. In *Death in the Afternoon*, Hemingway wrote,

> If a writer of prose knows enough about what he is writing
> about he may omit things that he knows and the reader, if the
> writer is writing truly enough, will have a feeling of those things
> as strongly as though the writer had stated them. The dignity
> of movement of an ice-berg is due to only one-eighth of it be-
> ing above water (192).

In Carver's fiction, it does seem that only one-eighth of the story
is "above water." The rest of what happens is beneath the surface.
It's that structure—in which so much is hidden from the reader
and yet somehow also known—that dictates the elements of the
minimalist style.

A Changing Culture

Having read "Cat in the Rain" and a Carver story or two, students
can begin to discover for themselves what the elements of
minimalist prose are. I like to fill the chalkboard with the phrases
they call out, and the first I hear is always "It's short!" That's certainly one of the most striking characteristics of minimalist fiction—and one of the things that makes it so appealing to high
school readers. My students chuckle a bit guiltily when I point
that out to them, but what I want them to understand is that this
abbreviated length *is* one of the reasons why minimalist writing
attained such popularity in the last decades of the twentieth century.

We discuss how life changed in the United States from the
late sixties onward and how we've become a society tempted by a
wide array of recreational activities, with reading low on the list.
We talk of the growth of malls and multiplex movie theaters, of
highly mobile two- and three-car families, of homes with televi-
sions in almost every room. We reflect on the impact technology
has had on our leisure time, on how many hours we spend watch-

ing videos, playing electronic games, talking on cell phones, and connecting to our computers. Although we are drawn to an increasing variety of activities in our free time, the ironic truth is that despite the conveniences of modern life we just don't have that much spare time anymore. Our lives are packed and programmed, and we run on schedules that leave us little time for literature. I also remind students of the changes brought about by the women's movement and explain how, as more women entered the workforce on a full-time basis, their leisure time diminished, while their children, shepherded into daycare and a myriad of lessons, clubs, and activities, also had less time to turn the pages of a book.

My students don't have to be convinced that they themselves are not eager readers, but typically they see that as a "teenage thing." Sometimes, at the beginning of a literature course, I'll send them out to survey people of various age groups to determine who's reading and who's not and to find out what is being read. Generally they come back surprised and maybe just a little troubled to find that even their elders aren't reading much more than the daily newspaper or the latest trendy magazine. If they need further proof of this, I can cite for them data from the 2002 Bureau of the Census Survey of Public Participation in the Arts. This project, done in conjunction with the National Endowment for the Arts, surveyed more than 17,000 American adults regarding their involvement in artistic pursuits, including reading. *Reading at Risk*, the report of that aspect of the survey, clearly indicates that literary reading is steadily declining in the United States, with "less than half of the American population now read[ing] literature" (NEA vii). The study stresses that "the accelerating declines in literary reading among all demographic groups of American adults indicate an imminent cultural crisis. . . . [A]t the current rate of loss, literary reading as a leisure activity will disappear in half a century" (xii).

From all of this, students can begin to understand why the minimalist style, reflected in a *short* short story, became so popular in the 1970s and 1980s. Carver's stories, like the fiction of such minimalists as Ann Beattie, Mary Robison, and Grace Paley, can be read in quick bursts, perhaps in the moments before bed or even while waiting in the gas line or in the dentist's office. It does not, however, I remind my students vehemently, make that literature of a lesser quality than that of the hefty classics. Writers write for a particular audience in a particular time. In the second half of the twentieth century, American culture underwent enormous changes, and the style of Carver and his contemporaries reflects the interests and values of that audience. Moreover, these minimalist writers, many of them quite young when they began to publish, were products of that time themselves and perhaps saw literature less as a "cold winter night by the fire" diversion and more as a way to comment on our culture. Certainly, too, as MFA and other writing programs began to flourish in major universities all over the United States, a phenomenon of the 1980s, budding writers studied under established names like Carver and, as eager students in every field do, absorbed aspects of their "master's" style.

The Minimalist Style

As a class, we then dig more deeply into what this style involves: "If the end result is a truly *short* story, how does the writer manage to achieve that length and still tell a complete story?" I ask my students.

Now comes a volley of new ideas to fill the board.

"He uses short words!" someone says, and this is quickly demonstrated by the fact that *flowerpot* might be the longest word in "Little Things."

"And short sentences." Sara offers lines as proof:

> Oh, oh, she said looking at the baby.
> He moved towards her.
> For God's sake! she said. She took a step back into the kitchen.
> I want the baby. (153)

And short words and short sentences, they all agree, lead to short paragraphs and finally a short story.

From this understanding of the minimalist structure, we can begin to discern other qualities of the style. Short words typically reflect a simple vocabulary. My students determine that the most difficult word in "Little Things" is *scuffle*. Often with simple vocabulary we see an equally simple sentence structure of the basic subject-predicate variety: "But he would not let go. He felt the baby slipping out of his hands and he pulled back very hard" (154). Minimalist writing uses little figurative language. Characters and setting are not *like* something else; they simply are. The characters—and typically there are few in a story—are rarely described in any depth or detail. As in "Little Things," they sometimes don't even have names. We know almost nothing about their backgrounds; we know them only in the *now*. It's common, in fact, for minimalist stories to be written entirely in the present tense. Much of what we do know about a character comes from our own almost intuitive understanding of that *type* of person in our society, and often the minimalist writer gives us our best clues through the use of brand names. A character who smokes Marlboros, wears Levis, and drives a Ford pickup is recognizable to any contemporary reader, especially to teenagers, who are very literate in the language of labels.

Just as characters are created with minimal detail, so too is action kept to a minimum. I do have students who complain that *nothing happens* in a Carver story, and in a sense they're right. Minimalist stories aren't action packed. They describe instead the tiny moments of a life, the ones that seem to matter only when one looks back. There are no complicated plots and no thundering dramatic moments when all action seems to hang in the balance. Even the most wrenching moments—the moment, for example, that a baby becomes a victim in its parents' hands—are described in cool, nonemotive tones, a kind of 1970s and eighties voice of detached indifference. It's a voice that hearkens back to that of the absurdists and existentialists but that has its own peculiar flavor, a result of the disenchantment and disillusionment Americans experienced as they struggled to make sense of the assassinations of the sixties, the turmoil of the Vietnam War, and the scandal of Watergate. It's a nihilistic voice and one that we continue to hear in fiction today. It's a voice that recognizes the near impossibility of happy endings and the difficulty, but necessity, of speaking the unhappy truth. One of the mottos of minimalist fiction is "Tell it like it is," and that's what Carver does.

But he doesn't always tell us everything, and that's where my students diverge in their opinion of minimalist writing. It's not unusual for a minimalist story to end with what students regard as no ending at all. Concluding lines such as "In this manner, the issue was decided" ("Little Things" 154), "'It has to do with Scotty, yes'" ("The Bath" 56), or "He said, 'I just want to say one more thing.' But then he could not think what it could possibly be"

("One More Thing" 151) are lines that leave the reader slightly mystified—and sometimes more than slightly frustrated. Some students love these open endings (in a review, one of my students called Carver's work "the most entertaining puzzle I've ever had to put together"), while others struggle with the vagueness, feeling almost cheated. But such ambiguous endings do have a purpose.

"So what does it mean—this lack of resolution?" I ask.

"Carver just wants to drive us crazy," Kevin declares. He might as well have thrown his hands up in a gesture of defeat. Some of his classmates nod.

But others are willing to dig deeper.

"Maybe he doesn't know what happens," someone offers.

"OK. Why?" I prompt. "Why no clear-cut conclusion?"

"Because life doesn't work that way." The words come from Teresa, and her voice, just a bit flat and weary, echoes with the tone of these minimalist stories. "Because there aren't any simple endings."

This my students understand. The world Carver creates is a world they know well. It's a world where there are no easy answers, no tidy conclusions, and no guaranteed happy endings. Maybe the couple in "Little Things" will kiss and make up, but it's just as likely they'll tear their lives to pieces as they tear their baby's arms apart. The point is, no matter how bad the choices we make may be, *we go on*. We turn another page and life takes another turn.

Modeling Minimalism

Minimalist fiction appears deceptively simple in both style and content. I always have students who, having read a few Carver stories, are convinced, "I could do that." I like to put them to the challenge, partly to demonstrate to them that what seems simple on the surface often is complex underneath. But more important, I want my students to model the minimalist style because, in many respects, it's a writing style with all the hallmarks of good writing. I remind them of another maxim of minimalism: "Less is more."

In his book *On Writing Well*, William Zinsser states,

> But the secret of good writing is to strip every sentence to its cleanest components. Every word that serves no function, every long word that could be a short word, every adverb that carries the same meaning that's already in the verb, every passive construction that leaves the reader unsure of who is doing what—these are the thousand and one adulterants that weaken the strength of a sentence. (7–8)

Zinsser could be celebrating minimalist writing with these words. Carver's most minimalist stories, particularly those published in his 1981 collection *What We Talk About When We Talk About Love*, all provide striking examples of stripped down sentences, simple vocabulary, and straightforward description.

Reminding them of these characteristics, I set my students to writing a piece in the minimalist style. I tell them the piece may be truth or fiction—or a Carveresque blend of the two—and the only requirement in terms of content is that it must focus on a human interaction. They see this as an easy task at first, and then, as they get into the writing, they begin to recognize the paradox: it is difficult to write simply. This is an excellent exercise particularly for those students who litter their writing with complex, convoluted sentences, elaborate and erroneous vocabulary gleaned from a thesaurus, and similar trappings of what they consider sophisticated, "adult" writing. This exercise teaches them that writers write for one purpose: to be understood. And Carver believed that passionately: "[I]n my view art is a linking between people, the creator and the consumer. Art is *not* self-expression, it is communication" (Bonetti 58).

Often my students surprise me with their skill in mastering the minimalist style and with the pleasure they take in this technique. Ashley invents the story of a young couple who, five years after the birth of their child, still have not found a way to reconcile their feelings for each other. Like Carver, she needs to say very little, and yet, as this excerpt shows, the story of this couple is very clear.

> ". . . Annie?" he pleaded.
> "Look, I'm feeling sorry right now and I know I shouldn't be. I told you Lizy and I made a new life for ourselves. You should've expected it." She felt exhausted and knew if he was there much longer she would do something irrational, the way things used to be with him. But look how things ended up. She loved her daughter. She would do this for her.
> "Please just go."
> He wouldn't let her shut the door.
> "I'm in love with him now," she said.
> He saw the door being shut on his face. He felt hatred for himself building up inside him. He walked slowly down the short driveway. It felt about three times longer than it was. . . .
> —*Ashley Martin, from "Who Lost?"*

Tim adopts the minimalist style in a nonfiction piece about a visit back to his beloved California. He opens with a description of the start of that journey:

> They say, "home is where the heart is," and if that's true, I left mine 3000 miles away in San Diego. Ever since I got off the

plane in Massachusetts, I've counted the days until I would be getting back on it and heading home. It was Christmas when I got my ticket back, with my mom. We left the following week. On the plane I listened to every CD that reminded me of living in California. Songs that used to make me homesick I blared until I noticed that half the plane was nodding to Tupac and Biggie. . . .

We got our luggage from the baggage claim. My mom put her four bags on a cart. I put on my backpack and carried my surfboard. We met up with my friends Garrett and Tony outside the airport and made a beeline for the nearest taco shop. It was just like old times. . . .

—*Tim Cunningham, from "Caught"*

The piece continues, describing a little trouble the three boys get into as they celebrate their California reunion. Throughout is the flavor of Carver with that burly "guy" voice that makes male students especially warm to him. Yet as distinctly masculine as Carver's voice is, he does not shy away from emotion. Carver's characters *feel*, and he makes the reader share their pain, yet he never cheapens human emotion by sentimentalizing or romanticizing. This is another strength of his writing and one that adolescent writers would do well to model. Some students do it so well that they become the models themselves.

Such is the case with Dan, author of "The Sleeper." This was a piece that stunned me when I read it for the first time a few years ago, and it continues to stun my students when I read it each year to them. "The Sleeper" is a brilliant example of minimalist writing in terms of its structure and style, but it is its content that so powerfully captures what Carver does best. "The Sleeper" describes what is, on the surface, a minor moment in a family interaction, and yet that moment represents so much more, especially in the heart of the protagonist.

The Sleeper

It was about three o'clock. He was getting tired. He wanted to sleep now; he slept a lot. He was happy this way. He was sick of thinking about his day in school—who he talked to, what girls looked at him, it was all too much. It was time to sleep. He woke up about four thirty because his mother was there. She came home from work early and sat at the end of the couch, where his feet were. He looked at the clock and then looked at her with a scowl. She had his senior pictures in her hands. She passed them over to him and he looked. They were no good, something a little wrong with each one.

"Your smile is so crooked," she agreed.

"It's the way I smile."

"Why can't you smile nice?"

"It's the way I smile."

"We can have retakes."

"I don't want to go through that again."

"You're much more handsome than this," she insisted.

"Great."

He'd been hearing compliments like this for as far back as he could remember and they meant nothing anymore.

"Your room is a mess," she interrupted his peace.

"What the hell does that have to do with anything!?"

"Don't talk like that, don't swear."

"I'll do what I please."

"You'll do what I say. I'm your mother." He had also heard statements like this for as far back as he could remember.

"You sleep too much," she broke the pause.

"I'm happy when I sleep."

At this time his sister walked into the room and picked up the pictures from the table they rested on. "Your smile is crooked." She forced herself into the situation, something that didn't need to happen.

"Shut the **** up!" he yelled and looked at them. They both looked hurt. He hurt them by yelling that one thing that shouldn't have been yelled, that they didn't need to hear. It happened too much like this, and not just with them, with everyone. It was now over, the whole situation. It never had to come to that. He knew it. He looked at the clock again and went into his room. He put his head down on the bed and went to sleep, where everyone was happy.

—*Dan McPhee*

What Dan captures—and what readers recognize—in this piece is the sense of alienation human beings feel even when surrounded by those closest to them. Even in his later stories, those of *Cathedral* (1983) and *Where I'm Calling From* (1988), when Carver's style grew more expansive, he still always created characters who struggle with loneliness and a lack of connection. Though Carver's people are those of a blue-collar culture, in many respects quite different from the middle-class suburban students I teach, my students see the same sense of isolation and disconnection in the people around them, and perhaps in themselves. What Carver makes students understand is that it is the essential sense of alienation in contemporary life that, paradoxically, connects us all. In doing this, he gives teachers and students a place to begin discussion of what it means to be a human being in our modern world, and there begins the development of empathy.

Beyond Words

I like to take students beyond words on a page to explore this idea of alienation. Edward Hopper's paintings provide a perfect means for that exploration and allow students to see that artistic expression, whatever the medium, is often a study of the human condition. Edward Hopper (1882–1967) is considered one of America's foremost painters of the twentieth century, and his work, especially that which depicts the landscapes of cities and small towns and the people who inhabit these places, bears witness to a changing America. Sherry Marker, in her introduction to *Edward*

Hopper, a collection of sixty-seven Hopper plates, writes, "Hopper was the first painter to emphasize the dark side of America's pellmell growth, to dwell on the forms of human isolation and impersonality that accompanied the country's seemingly invincible progress and expansion" (6).

These paintings give students a strong visual sense of the same people, places, and emotions that Carver captures in his fiction. Among my favorites are *Room in Brooklyn* (1932), a painting of a woman, her back to the viewer, who sits alone at a window overlooking another apartment building; *Sunlight in a Cafeteria* (1958), in which a man and a woman sit at separate tables in an otherwise empty restaurant; and *Nighthawks* (1942), a work that most of my students have seen but have never thought much about. In this classic Hopper painting, "usually cited as the quintessential Hopper presentation of isolation" (Marker 65), four characters are pictured through a diner window, three seated at the counter. One customer sits alone, his back hunched. A couple, their faces to the viewer, are together yet apart, both seemingly lost in their own thoughts. The fourth person, the counterman, goes about his work. It is late night; the street is deserted. The play of light and dark, for which Hopper is known, emphasizes the sense of anonymity and emptiness. Not only are these "nighthawks" cut off from one another, but they're somehow cut off from us, the viewers, as well. We can't quite infiltrate their lonely space, and yet we want very much to know their stories.

"So," I say to my students, "tell us their stories. Is the couple fighting? About to break up? Who's the man who sits alone? Should we fear him? Or tell us what the woman at the window in Brooklyn is thinking, or why the two restaurant patrons seem so distant, as if they're in two different universes. Create their stories, or maybe write their monologues. Give us the truth of their world."

This world of make-believe may seem an easy one to enter, but what students discover as they attempt to break through the windows that Hopper often puts his characters behind is that in order to write realistic stories, they have to penetrate not only glass walls but human walls as well. Hopper's people, like Carver's, tell us only so much; they leave us to fill in the spaces and to bring to the story our own experiences and feelings as human beings in an increasingly complex, and often cold, world. Many of the characteristics of minimalist fiction—from the coolly realistic settings to the aching but unexpressed emotion, from the comfortable familiarity of common characters and brand names (my students are particularly fond of the Ex-Lax sign in Hopper's *Drug Store!*) to the menacing undercurrent of mystery, from the immediacy of the present scene to the unresolved ambiguity of its outcome—are reflected in Hopper's paintings. As they create lives for Hopper's subjects, students, especially visual learners, can find another door into Carver's world.

Visual learners in particular can make strong connections between minimalist art and minimalist writing. The minimalist movement in art began in the United States in the late 1950s and was a reaction against the emotionalism of abstract expressionism. (A similar situation gave rise to minimalist writing, which, in its highly realistic portrayal of contemporary life, was in part a reaction against the experimental fiction of the 1960s.) Sculpture and installation are the primary modes of minimalist art; however, painting, most notably the work of Frank Stella (1936–), also demonstrates the minimalist movement. As with minimalist writing, the intent is to strip the work down to its most basic elements. For artists this means reducing the work to a focus on shapes, often in geometric patterns, and using the most fundamental materials, frequently industrial materials such as brick, aluminum, and steel. In the repetition, the simplicity, and, some might say, the tedium of the art, the artist presents a restrained, unemotional work that reflects the same sense of alienation evoked in minimalist fiction. The artist gives only so much; it's up to the viewer to bring to the work whatever more he or she chooses.

One piece of minimalist art that virtually all students are familiar with is Maya Lin's (1959–) Vietnam Veterans Memorial, which offers an excellent introduction to the examination of minimalist art. After viewing the memorial, students can talk about its design—the stark, black cut stone; the positioning of the monument in the earth; the simple listing of names; and the impact of the viewer's participation. Because they understand the extraordinary power the monument has, students recognize the truth of the minimalist motto "Less is more." In a design that embodies the elements of minimalist art—reduction, repetition, and restraint—Lin makes us see truth: the human cost of war, the lasting grief of death, and the sorrow that unites us all.

With a basic understanding of the concepts of minimalist art, students can undertake a project exploring the work of a specific minimalist artist. This project works best when students work in small groups, especially if their knowledge of art is limited. It's often helpful if the teacher provides a list of artists for students to research. Along with Stella, other important minimalists include installation artist Sol LeWitt (1928–), painter-sculptor Eva Hesse (1936–1970), and sculptors Donald Judd (1928–1994), Richard Serra (1939–), and Carl Andre (1935–). (Andre is of special interest in that his art also involves a series of poems written between the 1950s and the 1970s.) With easy access to visual images of art on various Web sites, students can see—and present to their classmates—the work of these artists. After each group has presented its artist, including biographical information, display and discussion of important pieces, and critical commentary, the class as a whole can pool this information to reach a real understanding of the concept of minimalist art, and students can see clearly its relationship to minimalist writing. At the same time, they come to understand how cultural changes influence the work of artists in all areas and how art, whatever form it may take, is an expression of the human condition.

I'd be happy teaching an entire course on minimalism, and I think many of my students would be quite happy taking that course too. For that reason, I regret that Carver rejected the term *minimalist*, with its intimation of "smallness of vision and execution" (Simpson and Buzbee 44). To me, there's nothing small about the vision of the minimalist artists. I believe they remind us of the hard truth about what it means to be a human being in these contemporary times. But perhaps it's that label, that attempt to *categorize* creative work, that's distasteful to an artist. As teachers and students, we find it efficient to lump together the work of those we study in order to see the connections, understand the influences, and make sense of the changes and developments. Certainly Carver's writing fits the category of minimalism as it has been defined by literary scholars. But Carver's work came first, before the category was defined and the label was listed. He was not trying to be a minimalist; he did not adopt the style because it was the fashion of the day. Rather, he wrote in a voice and style that reflected his unique view of the world. We are indebted to him for giving us that view and that voice, but perhaps we cannot demand that he stay in a box labeled "minimalist." Perhaps no artist should be limited in that way, because the essence of art is to defy the limits.

Further Resources

- Among the Web sites with information on Hopper's work is www.artchive.com/artchive/H/hopper.html.

- In his essay "American Light" published in *Remembering Ray* (William L. Stull and Maureen P. Carroll, eds.), Robert Coles writes of teaching Carver's works in a seminar he designed that combines the work of Carver and Hopper in an examination of American working-class culture. Coles also discusses the Hopper connection in the film *To Write and Keep Kind* (Walkinshaw).

- Hopper's *Nighthawks* has also been connected to Hemingway's "The Killers," published in *Scribner's Magazine* in March 1927. Hopper was a fan of Hemingway's fiction (Marker 65), and some believe that the story, the tale of two hired gunmen who wait for their prey to enter a diner, may have been inspiration for this painting.

- The work of other minimalist writers can also be connected to that of particular artists. I like to pair Ann Beattie's fiction with the floating figures of Marc Chagall (1887–1985), whom she makes reference to in her short story "Sunshine and Shadow." The mothers and daughters frequently seen in Mary Robison's stories can be connected to the art of Mary Cassatt (1844–1926), a reference Robison makes in her short story "What I Hear."

- Web images of the Vietnam Veterans Memorial can be found at www.nps.gov/vive/home.htm, http://thewall-usa.com or www.viewthewall.com.

Interlude: Outside Looking In

■ ■

This is a story of a boy and a teacher. It is a short story, a seemingly simple story. It is a story without an ending. It is, I suppose, a minimalist story.

Some years ago a boy sat in my classroom. He seemed not to be an extraordinary boy or an exceptional boy. Courteous, quiet, attentive, he was a regular boy. He didn't stand out. He didn't stand out until the day we began to read the stories of Raymond Carver, and the boy, who liked these stories, began to write. And then one day his paper tumbled out of a pile of student stories, and with his first few lines, the boy became someone special. He became Dan—and he was a writer.

Raymond Carver taught, albeit reluctantly, in university writing programs for part of his life, but he never had to set foot in my classroom to become one of the most powerful teachers this boy Dan ever had. Before he read Carver's work, Dan never thought of himself as a writer. He was a good student, but he wasn't a writer and he had never tried to be one. And then, like so many young writers before him, inspired by Carver's voice and the minimalist style, Dan began to experiment with words, and the pieces he produced astounded me. It wasn't just imitation Carver. The voice had a unique edge and attitude, a nineties nuance, that hummed with the ghost of Carver but spoke with the spirit of Dan.

The following September Dan went off to college to pursue a major that didn't leave much time for writing stories. I sent him with admonitions not to waste his writing talent, but I worried that without encouragement he'd lose faith in his ability and maybe even forget the joy writing brought him. I half expected him to simply disappear, and, in that way all teachers learn, I let him go from my mind.

But he didn't disappear. Every once in a while he'd arrive in an envelope or on my e-mail screen. Sometimes he'd show up in a story, a piece that he was writing not for a class but for himself, and he'd be eager for feedback. Often, feeling the pressure of his course work and the distractions of college life, he'd bemoan the fact that he didn't have time for writing fiction, and I'd remind him that living is a part of writing too, that you have to experience the world to ever put it on paper. I wasn't worried anymore. I realized that this was a boy who, like Carver himself, could not go back. He was a boy who would always have to write.

Dan graduated and left soon after to cross the country for California and all the prospects the "Go West, young man" ideal has always had to offer. Before he left, there was a flurry of e-mails between us as I told him about the book I was writing on Carver and asked for his permission to use a piece of his writing in it. He was generous with his encouragement of the project and, perhaps unknowingly, quieted some of my concerns that there might be those who wouldn't see Carver as an important writer to use in a high school classroom. He wrote,

> Yours was the only high school class where the readings didn't fall along the straight and narrow. Everything prior to your class was by a noted author and/or was considered a "classic,"

which isn't necessarily a bad thing, but it's not as valuable as being introduced to many different authors, genres, and ideas.

Then he talked about his plans for California.

It's been hard trying to write in this environment of constant academic and social activity. So hopefully I'll be able to take a step back in California and get something out because I have plenty to write about—I just need to be outside the situations looking in, instead of directly inside them.

I couldn't help but think of Carver, not much older than Dan and in his own corner of California, trying as desperately to write but caught in a very different set of circumstances, surrounded by his wife and children, burdened by financial responsibilities, dependent on alcohol, yet struggling to get outside the situation long enough to create in his fiction what it felt like inside.

I haven't heard from Dan since he left. I'm imagining him in San Diego or maybe Los Angeles making a life filled with new faces and new challenges. And I'm imagining him finally finding the time and the distance to re-create the place and people he left behind.

But a funny thing happened, a strange coincidence of sorts. I was running a workshop for teachers recently, and a participant mentioned to me that his nephew had been in my class. "He said you were his best teacher," the gentleman said smiling.

Who can decline such a compliment? I thanked him for telling me so. "And who's your nephew?" I asked.

"Dan McPhee," he said, and so I had to smile and shake my head.

"That wasn't me," I said. "That was Raymond Carver."

3 Revision: A Not-So-Small, Good Thing

I know vaguely where I'm going. And then I write the first draft or rough draft so rapidly that I don't stop and take care of the niceties. . . . I try to do the story once in maybe thirty-five or forty pages, in longhand, knowing I'll have to go back, and that the real work will begin later after I get it typed up. And then it's not at all uncommon to do ten or fifteen drafts, twenty drafts of that story. And then I find myself changing it, maybe even after it's been published. (Carver qtd. in Pope and McElhinny 15)

We're working on revision. For inspiration, I read these words of Raymond Carver to my students—and they groan. Ten or twenty drafts? They make it clear that three is the most I should ever expect. Revision *after* publication? Isn't that like rewriting after the grade is recorded? The affection my students feel for Carver seems to falter a bit, but—I can almost see them remind themselves—he hasn't let them down so far, so . . . they sigh and give him—and me—a chance. All right, their expressions say, let's talk about revision.

Student writers hate to revise, and all writing teachers know how hard it is to convince them that revision is at the heart of good writing. Carver can be an impressive ally in that struggle, for not only did Carver revise his work extensively *before* publication, but he also frequently *re*published stories in new and revised forms. Because of this practice, students have the opportunity to see various versions of the same story in published pages, and, by examining these altered stories, they can see vividly the power of revision.

This chapter looks at two Carver stories—"The Bath" and "Everything Stuck to Him"—and their revised (and, in a sense, revived) counterparts—"A Small, Good Thing" and "Distance." Through these examples, students can see how critical the act of revision is, and how the smallest—and the not-so-small—choices a writer makes can have an enormous impact on a story.

Reseeing Revision

I have a theory about revision. While we certainly need to teach students how to revise, giving them techniques to expedite that process, we first need to convince them that revision matters and that it's as fundamental to the writing process as the act of composing. It's true that revision can be painstaking and difficult, and it may never bring the same sense of exhilaration the writer feels when his or her words first burst on to the page. But revision *is* writing, and many writers, Carver included, find it a pleasurable challenge.

> I like to mess around with my stories. I'd rather tinker with a story after writing it, and then tinker some more, changing this, changing that, than have to write the story in the first place. . . . Maybe I revise because it gradually takes me into the heart of what the story is *about*. I have to keep trying to see if I can find that out. It's a process more than a fixed position. ("On Rewriting" 108–9)

Too many students, however, see revision not as an essential part of the process but rather as a sort of punishment. When a teacher/reader offers critical feedback or proposes a revision, the student often interprets that as, "I guess I must have done it wrong, so now I've got to figure out how do it right." I honestly believe many students think that "real" writers, the Raymond Carvers of the world, simply "do it right" the first time. My theory is that if we can convince our students that revision has very little to do with right or wrong but is rather about *making choices*, then we can get them to do it, maybe even with enthusiasm.

I tell my students that "right" and "wrong" come in the editing phase, that final cleanup of the piece when we check for spelling errors, grammar flaws, and mistakes in punctuation. But revision is something very different, and its meaning is inherent in the word itself: *re-vision / re-seeing*. Carver learned this from his mentor John Gardner, who believed "that a writer found what he wanted to say in the ongoing process of *seeing* what he'd said. And this seeing, or seeing more clearly, came about through revision" ("John Gardner" 110).

In the revision phase, the writer looks candidly at her or his material with fresh, new eyes, and with that new vision makes decisions about how to reshape, rework, and rewrite the words so that they say precisely what is in the writer's mind. Sometimes it's a matter of changing a word or a line, or maybe many words and lines. It might be that the story should start where it ends and that the last paragraph should become the first. Sometimes the point of view needs to be altered. Perhaps certain details should be added while others should be omitted, and maybe that section written as summary should be played out in dramatic detail, perhaps even with dialogue. It's likely the piece will grow—or shrink —and sometimes the whole work will find its way to the wastebasket, a false start that gives birth to something much better. This, I tell my students, is what we mean by revision, and though a few groan even more loudly because *this* kind of revision is more difficult than correcting a misspelled word or moving a misplaced semicolon, others are intrigued because revision now too becomes an act of creation.

Significant revisions can be big or small. In his essay "On Writing," Carver cites a line from Isaac Babel's short story "Guy de Maupassant" in which "the narrator has this to say about the writing of fiction: 'No iron can stab the heart with such force as a period put just at the right place'" ("On Writing" 89–90). Writers know the power of a period, and I always encourage students to remember that the tiniest revision may have the most impact. But it isn't always easy to teach young writers how to make these very delicate but effective changes, so I typically try to tackle first the bigger, broader sorts of changes students might make in their pieces. No changes are so dramatic as those seen between Carver's "The Bath" and "A Small, Good Thing," most strikingly in their endings, and so these stories offer an outstanding illustration of the effect revision can have on a piece of writing.

A Tale of Two Stories

"The Bath" was published in *What We Talk About When We Talk About Love* (1981); "A Small, Good Thing" was published in a summer 1982 edition of the literary journal *Ploughshares* and later in the collections *Cathedral* (1983) and *Where I'm Calling From* (1988). The former story is about a third the length of its later counterpart. Students need only thumb through both stories to realize that there's much more to "A Small, Good Thing," and as they do so, their interest is piqued.

"How can pretty much the same story be so short and so long?" John asks.

I give a little shrug. "Apparently Carver had more things to say in one version," I say. "More detail maybe."

"Then let's read the short one," John says, and there is general laughter. They've become devoted fans of minimalism very quickly!

"OK," I say. "Put 'A Small, Good Thing' away. We'll read 'The Bath.'" Surprised glances circle the room, but I don't have to tell students twice.

And so we read "The Bath." In the story, almost-eight-year-old Scotty is hit by a car on the morning of his birthday as his mother plans a celebration complete with a cake decorated with a spaceship and made by a local baker. As Scotty's parents sit tensely by his hospital bedside, their son in a sort of coma, all thoughts of the birthday and the cake are forgotten. Their anxiety is heightened by the ominous and anonymous phone calls that come each time one of them goes home to feed the dog, have a rest, or take a bath. The story ends with one final telephone call.

"'It is about Scotty,' the voice said. 'It has to do with Scotty, yes'" ("The Bath" 56).

"That's it?" John says incredulous as we read these last lines. "So who is it?"

"Yeah, and what happened to Scotty?" a student asks.

I give another shrug. "I don't know," I say. "That's the end."

The room erupts into conversation.

My students have a love-hate relationship with this story. They are mesmerized by it. It has a haunting tone, a bit reminiscent of the best horror stories, and they can argue forever about whether the voice is the doctor delivering news, the baker wanting his money, or perhaps the hit-and-run driver admitting responsibility for Scotty's injuries. Despite their fascination with the work, the ending drives them crazy. Inevitably they beg me to tell them who is calling, and the more I try to explain that it isn't a puzzle, that there's no hidden answer that I'm privy to, the more frustrated they become. The story itself is a model of minimalist writing, offering virtually no detail about anything. We know little about Scotty's family save that there is a mother and a father. The accident is described quickly and dispassionately and with a typical Carveresque twist as Scotty's companion, after witnessing his friend fall to the curb, "stood holding the potato chips. He was wondering if he should finish the rest or continue on to school" (48). The hospital scenes are flat and almost coldly impersonal, peopled only by "the doctor," "the nurse," and another mother, only briefly referred to, who waits for word on her son Nelson. We never even find out if Scotty lives or dies.

Until we read "A Small, Good Thing." And I don't have to twist any arms to get my students to now do that. Eagerly they reach for this story, sure that the answers they're looking for are in its pages—and they're right. In this lengthy revision of "The Bath" there is much more descriptive material, including details about the parents, Ann and Howard Weiss ("Until now, his life had gone smoothly . . . the advanced degree in business, a junior partnership in an investment firm. Fatherhood . . .") ("A Small, Good Thing" 379); about the hospital personnel ("The doctor [Dr. Francis] was a handsome, big-shouldered man with a tanned face. He wore a three-piece blue suit, a striped tie, and ivory cuff links. His gray hair was combed along the side of his head, and he looked as if he had come from a concert") (382); and even about the baker ("The baker was not jolly. . . . He made her [Ann] feel uncomfortable, and she didn't like that. . . . [S]he studied his coarse features and wondered if he'd ever done anything else with his life besides be a baker") (376–77). There's an extended scene in the hospital waiting room in which Ann interacts with her almost-double, a woman here named Evelyn, who is awaiting news of her son, now called Franklin, who has been critically injured in a stabbing. Most significant, at least in my students' minds, in "A Small, Good Thing" Scotty dies, a sudden shocking death, one that always takes readers by surprise.

But the story does not end there, and my students hungrily read the last nine pages of this version. Those phone calls are an integral part of this story too, and the final pages reveal who the voice on the other end of the phone is. My students, the ones who have guessed "right," cheer when they learn it's the baker. They then read a final poignant scene in which, overcome by grief coupled with fury at what she sees as the baker's insensitivity (though he has no idea at the time he's making the calls that the birthday boy is dying), Ann and her husband go to the bakery late at night to confront the baker. There, in a curious moment of redemption with shared words and cinnamon rolls, the three of them find something like peace. Not happiness, of course—"Remember," I tell my students, "this *is* a Carver story,"—but something closer to grace than could ever be found in Carver's earlier works, particularly, in this case, "The Bath."

We spend a lot of time, my students and I, debating which story is better. In a class of twenty-four, the vote is often split down the middle, and that, I tell them, says something about revision. Had one of these stories been absolutely "better," we likely would have known it. Most of us would have voted for it and viewed the other as a badly written draft. But that's not the case.

"I like 'The Bath' better," Jess declares. "I like making up my own ending. I like not knowing for sure."

"Nah," says Ben. "That's just dumb. The author's supposed to tell you what happened. Hey, what if Carver didn't even know?!"

They think about that for a minute. Does a writer have to "know" how his story ends? And if he doesn't, what does that mean?

John's not giving up on the strengths of strict minimalism. "I just like the shorter one better," he says. "Who needs a lot of words? We got most of the same story in the first version. Who cares what the doctor was wearing?"

We could argue all day—and usually we do spend an entire period debating the merits of one version over the other. Through that discussion, students come to realize that both stories are "right" in terms of quality. Both "work," and both attract their share of admirers. Students see then that revision is an *experiment*, in a sense. It's an opportunity for writers to let their material take new shape, new substance, and new soul, and it's through revision that writers find what it is they really want to say.

My students always want to know what it was that Carver wanted to say, but the story behind "The Bath" and "A Small, Good Thing" is a complicated one, and one about which the truth is not absolutely clear. Some Carver scholars maintain that "The Bath" reflects Carver's vision in a particular period of his life, a time in which he was developing a sort of "signature" style and battling demons that made him see the world as the dark and threatening place it is painted to be in this story. But there's also evidence suggesting that Carver preferred a version like "A Small, Good Thing" all along but that he allowed his editor, Gordon Lish, to override his own preferences and to edit a longer original version for the sake of publication. Carver himself offers a rather ambiguous explanation in a 1984 interview in which he comments on the two stories:

> Certainly there's a lot more optimism in "A Small Good Thing."
> . . . I went back to that one . . . because I felt there was unfin-
> ished business that needed attending to. The story hadn't been
> told originally; it had been messed around with, condensed

and compressed in "The Bath" to highlight the qualities of men-ace that I wanted to emphasize. . . . But I still felt there was unfinished business, so . . . I went back to "The Bath" and tried to see what aspects of it needed to be enhanced, redrawn, reimagined. (McCaffery and Gregory 69)

Though my students are frustrated, again wanting absolute answers and explanations, I remind them that writing is an art and that the artist can't always explain how his or her work came into being. But I also tell them that this may serve as a good illus-tration of how important it is for writers to remember that they own the words and that it's their name that will go on those words should they reach publication. For that reason, I say, it's impor-tant to understand that whatever feedback you as a writer re-ceive—from a teacher, a response group member, or ultimately an editor—it's *your* choice as the writer to decide whether to imple-ment that advice. Writing is all about decision making, and every suggestion you receive has to be considered carefully. I tell my students too that I honestly don't think it matters how or why there came to be two versions of Carver's story. I'm just glad there are these two stories because through them we can see how the same basic plot line, the same central characters, and even a very similar writing style can be reworked and revised—*re-seen*—and two very different pieces of writing can result. Both good, very good.

This is my response to reluctant revisers who say of their own work, "Oh, it's good enough," when I encourage them to rewrite. "Yes," I tell such students, "it is good enough. But it could be different." And somehow, focusing on the fact that it could be different—not better—gives them the encouragement and the courage they need to tackle revision. I know they expect me to tell them it could be better, but those words are daunting because the truth is, most students do the best they can. As teachers we all know students' writing could be better, but students aren't sure how to make it better or they would have done so from the start. But tell them to make a piece *different*, and they're usually willing to try. When they're done making it different, often they discover they've made it better too.

Directing Revision

Frequently I direct revision with my students. I ask them to bring in their most recent drafts, and then I offer them some choices. "Add a character," I might say if they're writing fiction. Or "Revamp the ending by adding a scene or ending the story earlier." If they're writing essays, I might ask them to use scissors to physically cut the essay into its separate paragraphs. I tell them to rearrange the paragraphs in a different order and then to tape the whole together while considering new transitions. When students write poetry, I'll have them do the same with lines, forcing the poem into a new shape, or I might tell them they can't use any words beginning with *m* or maybe *p* and so make them experiment with new language. Always I tell them that this next draft may not be a *better* draft but that it will be a *different* draft and that it will hopefully offer the writer a new way of seeing some aspect of her or his writing. This sort of revision activity may seem forced or it may seem more like play, but it's important work because it makes students understand what revision really is. It's *re-seeing* the whole.

Another revision idea that I use for all types of writing and find especially effective comes straight from the minimalist school. Carver, like many minimalist writers, typically begins his stories at a crisis point. There's very little introductory material; readers simply find themselves in the action of the story within the first few lines. So we read opening lines like:

> It had been two days since Evan Hamilton had stopped smoking, and it seemed to him everything he'd said and thought for the two days somehow suggested cigarettes. ("Bicycles, Muscles, Cigarettes" 21)

or

> L.D.'s wife, Maxine, told him to get out the night she came home from work and found L.D. drunk again and being abusive to Rae, their fifteen-year-old. ("One More Thing" 147)

This provides an excellent lesson for young writers, who often have difficulty getting into their stories. What writing teacher hasn't muddled through an opening paragraph (or two or three) before finally finding the real start of the piece, the place where the writer finds voice and focus? Often I ask students to write an entirely new opening for their piece after the complete work has been drafted. If they balk at this, I say, "OK, so find a point in the draft you've already written where the piece could begin instead." They do, and often that place is the start of the second paragraph or maybe the third, and suddenly they realize that that first paragraph, that often vague and vacuous first paragraph, can go. I tell them that when they wrote that paragraph, they were wading into the water; now they're ready to take the plunge and start the story with a splash.

Original opening
It was one of those stale fall nights last year. A past principal of my old middle school had passed away of a heart attack at an extremely young age. He left behind two kids and his pregnant wife. The funeral procession was to be held around 8:00 at the gymnasium of my old school. My father had let our dogs out

before we left. After about twenty minutes, only one came back, Koko. My one-year-old Golden, Duke, was still gone.

—*Rob Day*

Revised opening
Duke hadn't come home yet. Koko, the older one, had been home for a good twenty minutes. Being only about a year old, Duke, my Golden, liked to graze in the woods. I stood at the sliding glass door waiting to see his face and his tail wagging.

—*Rob Day*

Both his response group and I tell Rob that while the principal's death is likely an effective link to the sad story we expect to read about the disappearance of Duke, it simply gets too much play at the beginning and it starts the reader off in the wrong direction. That information might better fit in the next paragraph to explain why Rob and his family have to leave the house, and the tragedy of it will help to heighten the feeling of anxiety when the dog still does not appear. I suggest to Rob that his original first line is too much of what I call a "weather report" opening. Students have a tendency to start their stories with lines like "It was a sunny Saturday morning," or "It happened on a hot summer day," simply because such a line helps them find their way into the story. Though Rob uses a great adjective in the word *stale*, the opening line doesn't grab a reader's attention, whereas the revised first line— "Duke hadn't come home yet"—certainly does. With that line, Rob jumps feet first into his story.

Small Changes

"Everything Stuck to Him" and its revision "Distance" offer students another way to approach a story, as well as giving teachers more opportunity to teach the value of revision. These two stories both use the device of the frame. They open with the narrator, a typical Carver father, being asked by his adult daughter, a woman whom he rarely sees, "what it was like when she was a kid" ("Everything Stuck to Him" 127). In a few brief paragraphs, the story travels from Milan, where father and daughter are meeting, back in time to "a little apartment under a dentist's office" (128), where two teenagers are struggling to establish the patterns of both their new marriage and parenthood. The story culminates in a moment of decision when the boy has to choose whether to put the needs of his wife and newborn daughter over his personal desires, in this case a hunting trip.

My students love this story, both versions. They like the teenage protagonists, both of whom are sympathetic characters, and they can empathize with the difficulty of making the kind of decisions that adulthood demands. "Everything Stuck to Him," published in *What We Talk About When We Talk About Love* (1981), is the more pared-down story. It lacks some of the detail of "Distance," published in *Fires* (1983) and *Where I'm Calling From* (1988), but the two stories are not as dramatically different as are the stories about Scotty. As such, then, these two stories allow students to see some of the finer aspects of revision.

In "Everything Stuck to Him," although the boy's dilemma revolves around the prospect of a hunting trip with a man named Carl, that specific activity seems almost inconsequential. The boy could be deciding to do anything that he loves doing, anything that will take him away for a time from his wife and his infant daughter. Certainly hunting is seen as a male, some might say macho, activity, and my students understand that in finally deciding not to go on this trip but rather to stay and help with his child, the boy is acknowledging that now, as a husband and father, he can't only be a hunter; he must also be a nurturer. But in "Distance," Carver gives greater meaning to the specific predicament the boy finds himself in when he focuses on the idea of killing Canada geese. The young wife asks the boy if they will always love each other.

> Always, the boy said. And we'll always be together. We're like the Canada geese, he said, taking the first comparison that came to mind, for they were often on his mind in those days. They only mate once. They choose a mate early in life, and they stay together always. If one of them dies or something, the other one will live by itself. ("Distance" 189)

The girl, saddened by this, asks if he has ever killed one of these geese. He tells her yes.

> You can't think about it when you're doing it. You see, I love everything there is about geese. I love to just watch them even when I'm not hunting them. But there are all kinds of contradictions in life. You can't think about the contradictions. (190)

In this revision, an addition that is minor in terms of length (approximately one page) but major in terms of material, Carver adds an element of symbolism as well as the use of foreshadowing that some might say enrich the story and give it a real poignancy. Of course, not everyone would say that. Certainly not all my students.

"That's stupid," says one of the boys in the back. "No eighteen-year-old kid would say that."

Some nod in agreement.

"He's being too nice," says one of the girls. "In the other story, he's not that nice."

Although that's not precisely fact, there is a kernel of truth in what she says for, in "Everything Stuck to Him," Carver doesn't give the boy—or his wife—much chance to speak. There's no conversation about love or death or even geese, and even in the most "emotional" scene, when the couple settles their disagreement, their words are truly minimal—and minimalist.

> Hey, the boy said.
> I'm sorry, the girl said.
> It's all right, the boy said
> I didn't mean to snap like that.
> It was my fault, he said.
> You sit down, the girl said. How does a waffle sound with bacon? ("Everything Stuck to Him" 133)

Minimal too is the material involving Carl in "Everything Stuck to Him." Carl is described only as "an old hunting friend of his [the boy's] father" (129). In a brief phone conversation, he offers congratulations on the birth of the baby, but he seems much more enthusiastic about the possibility of a hunting trip. Beyond that, Carl does not appear in the story, and, though the boy makes it as far as his own driveway before deciding not to go on the trip, he never makes further contact with Carl.

For many of my students, that's just fine. They don't believe they need to know any more about Carl.

"The story isn't about Carl," they say. "The point is, is the kid going to step up and do the right thing? Is he going to be a real father? Carl's just there to set up the mess the kid's in."

But when they read "Distance," they realize that the revised material involving Carl changes the situation.

> The boy liked Carl Sutherland. He'd been a friend of the boy's

father, who was dead now. After the father's death, maybe trying to replace a loss they both felt, the boy and Sutherland had started hunting together. . . . [T]he man had a toughness and woods-savvy about him that the boy liked and admired. ("Distance" 188)

"See, here it's not just about a hunting trip," they say. "This guy's like the kid's father. That means something."

And when I push them to explain what it means, they begin to discuss conflicting loyalties and obligations and what it means to be "family."

In "Distance," the boy wrestles longer with his decision. He drives as far as Carl's house, described in a line that gives my students pause when they reflect on the new title. "Driving, the boy looked out at the stars and was moved when he considered their distance" (193). Carl, who has been waiting for the boy, apologizes because he has just called the house and regrets that he has presumably awakened the wife. The boy explains that they've both been up because of the baby's crying: "I guess there's something wrong with the baby. I don't know. The baby keeps crying, I mean. The thing is, I guess I can't go this time, Carl" (194). Carl understands the choice the boy has made, and his final words are almost a sort of blessing: "You're a lucky boy and I mean that" (194).

"I like Carl," says Tina contentedly. This version *feels* better to her and to many other students. The pieces fit together and the whole seems more satisfying. They like getting to know the characters on the page. They like it when fiction doesn't quite so completely mimic life. And yet they still accept that in Carver's world things don't turn out well, and they are not surprised when Carver brings them back to the frame, to the almost estranged daughter—the baby grown up—and to the father who remembers that morning and a marriage that did not last.

> But he stays by the window, remembering that life. They had laughed. They had leaned on each other and laughed until the tears had come, while everything else—the cold and where he'd go in it—was outside, for a while anyway. (197)

This ending is virtually identical to the earlier ending of "Everything Stuck to Him." There are two very minor changes. Here in the revision Carver has added "that life" to the first line, and he has removed a comma that originally was placed after the word *cold*.

"He changed a *comma?*" someone says, skeptical about the need for such a change.

I remind them of Babel's line, "'No iron can stab the heart with such force as a period put just at the right place'" ("On Writing" 90), but it's still hard to persuade them that such minuscule changes matter. Yet, in comparing the content of these two Carver stories, they have become convinced that the material a writer chooses to put in or take out and the style in which the writer chooses to present it is of enormous importance and can change the tenor of a story.

What's in a Name?

A final example of seemingly small but certainly significant revision is seen in the titles of these stories. My students struggle to compose titles. Frequently I'm asked, "Does it *have* to have a title?" and though I tell them, yes, and emphasize how important a title can be to the understanding of the work, they're often apt to leave a big blank space where the title should be. These two stories offer a persuasive example of how much a title can matter. "Everything Stuck to Him" and "Distance": the two titles seem, in fact, almost opposite in meaning, the first implying a terrible closeness, the second its obvious extreme. Literally, what sticks to the young husband in both stories are the syrupy waffles and bacon that accidentally land in his lap as the couple, in a tender breakfast scene, make up after their argument about the hunting trip: "We won't fight anymore, she said. The boy said, We won't" ("Everything Stuck to Him" 134). But this is of course Carver Country, a land without happily-ever-after endings, and we need only read on a few paragraphs to reach the ending, the frame, and that final image of the cold.

"So what else stuck to him besides the waffles?" I ask my students.

They're quick to answer.

"His responsibilities."

"Fatherhood."

"Decisions."

"That's it?" I ask. "Just the hard stuff?"

Lindsay shakes her head. "No," she says. "The memories, the good times. They stuck to him too." She pauses. "And maybe his daughter? At least a little bit."

"So why, then, if there's so much stuck to him, did Carver call the later version 'Distance'?" I ask.

This takes a little longer, and their answers are more tentative.

"Because now he's looking back?"

"Because he and his wife didn't stay together?"

"Because he'll never really be close to his daughter?"

And usually there are a few who read closely and who want to know if the title has to do with those stars in the distance.

Clearly there are no definite answers, but in the two titles we see again the effect of revision. Each title emphasizes a different aspect of the story. My students think the first, "Everything Stuck to Him," implies a weight or burden but also a permanence that "Distance" does not.

"So are titles important?" I say. They nod.

"Remember," I tell them, "a title too can be revised. It may *have* to be revised after the story is written, when the writer has seen what it is he or she has to say."

Hearing the Heart

This is what revision is all about—discovering what it is you as a writer have to say. Often I'll ask students who think they're close to their final draft to write in a sentence or two what it is they intended to say in that piece. I'm not asking for a summary of the piece; I'm asking for a short statement of its meaning: "I meant to say that getting that tattoo changed me. It made me feel like I was independent." Or "I meant to say that my mother holds our family together and no one appreciates that." Sometimes students can tell for themselves by then rereading their drafts whether they have succeeded in accomplishing their goal. Sometimes they need the help of their response group to decide. When they realize they have fallen short of saying what it is they have to say, they're often discouraged, wanting to settle for saying whatever is already on the paper. But with encouragement and direction, most will persevere and revise their work until it does say what's in their head and in their heart.

Jason wrote a piece about driving too fast and hitting a neighbor's dog. The draft ended with the line "I turned the wheel to the left and hit the dog." His was a moving story, but through response it became clear that that wasn't the whole story Jason wanted to tell. He wanted to tell us that there are different levels of regret, and though he deeply regretted hitting the dog, what haunts him more is the fact that he didn't stop; he "slammed on the gas and headed home." Once Jason discovered that this is what he meant to say, he took a deep breath and said it, adding two paragraphs and much meaning to his story. In a written reflection sheet that students hand in with their final drafts, I asked, "What did you struggle with in writing this paper? How successful were you were at meeting this problem?" Jason's response:

> [I struggled most with] writing the part that I ran from the accident. I was successful, but it was hard to write down on paper. It brought back all those weird feelings again.

Those "weird feelings" were what made the story. They took Jason and his readers into a Carver kind of country, a "territory of the heart" (Caldwell 247). This, my students learn, is the real challenge of revision: coming to the truth and having the courage to speak it.

Further Resources

- The film *Short Cuts* (1993), directed by Robert Altman, is based on nine stories, including "A Small, Good Thing," and one poem by Carver. (The collection *Short Cuts* is published by Vintage Books [1993].) In the film, which Altman calls a sort of "Carver soup" (Stewart 3), the characters are transplanted to suburban Los Angeles. Altman often changes characters' names and their relationships to one another, and he moves characters from one story to another. Because of these changes, as well as the adult nature of the film, it may not be appropriate for classroom use, but teachers will find it an interesting approach to Carver's themes and ideas.

■ *Carve Magazine* (www.carvezine.com), an online literary journal from the University of Washington, was inspired by the work of Carver. The bimonthly journal accepts literary fiction only and sponsors an annual Raymond Carver Short Story Award. The Web site includes the text of a February 2001 interview with Tess Gallagher.

Interlude: Sustenance

■ ■

Eight days into the school year and I am in search of cinnamon buns. After the third grocery store stop, I am about to concede that the quest is futile. But I hear Raymond Carver in my head, "'Eating is a small, good thing in a time like this'" ("A Small, Good Thing" 404), and I think, oh yes, we need small, good things right now.

My students, the ones who will be reading Carver's story "A Small, Good Thing" tomorrow, are a weary bunch. Seniors, many of whom are less than stellar students struggling to make up credit for English courses they have failed, they look defeated—and it is only September. I bring them Raymond Carver stories as a sort of offering, and they perk up a bit. As one boy says, "Ray gets it." Ray "gets" that life is always hard and often hurtful, and when he writes of those who are simply "out"—out of love, out of money, out of work, out of hope—my students, even at seventeen, understand too well. But they don't read easily on their own, and sometimes, even when we read aloud in class, they don't bother to turn the pages. I ask them to write a personal essay about regret, something else Carver "got," and a few, charged by the topic, write feverishly, but others sit slumped and wordless in front of the computers. They're good kids, neither rude nor unruly, but I wonder if their quiet calm is a sign of a certain maturity—or simply weariness bred of disillusionment and the feeling that June, graduation, *life* is forever far away. All I can say is that they seem beaten, and mostly by an educational system that has never let them find success.

In these eight days we are getting to know one another. Anna tells me she adores horses. Or no, she doesn't tell me that exactly. She tells me that she was up until 2:00 a.m. soaking an abscess on her horse's leg and that then she had to return to the barn at 5:00 a.m. to begin her morning chores. But yes, she says when I press her, she adores horses—and she smiles the most beautiful smile. Marcus tells me this is his eighth school. Or no, he doesn't tell me that. He tells the other students when they look at him the first day and say, "Are you new?" He nods. "I'm always new," he says, and when they ask where else he has gone to school, he smiles halfheartedly. "Albania," he says, his words thickly accented. And before that Italy, but he never stays anywhere long. Andy tells me that he is an artist. Or no, he doesn't tell me that. But when I walk by his desk while we're reading Carver, he is drawing furiously, a collage of faces more striking than any I have ever seen. "Can I see more of your work?" I ask him after class, and the next day he brings me a sketchpad full. And George, George does tell me something. He tells me that the most memorable moment in his life was when he watched a good friend die.

These are my students. They are people who live hard lives but rich lives, lives of an intensity that their forlorn faces hide. But they don't live student lives. They should, I know that, but they don't. They don't do much homework or worry much about grades. They're not especially eager for a teacher's approval, nor do they feel any real need to know what teachers think they should know. What they do know is that all day long they are faced with adults who demand that they be students when what they are struggling to do first is survive.

So what can I give them? I can't remake them, nor can I remake the schools that have failed them. But I can give them Carver and cinnamon buns. Small, good things, I think, as I make my way down the bakery aisle. And there on the shelf sit three boxes of cinnamon buns. Though I wish I could bring my students homemade rolls, gooey and warm from the oven, these brand-name buns will have to do. I add two gallons of orange juice to my cart.

Tuesday morning first period. I hand out "A Small, Good Thing." I count four heads on the desks. Behind my desk is the grocery bag. I had planned to save the buns and juice until the end of class, a reward for finishing the story, for reaching the final scene, in which, over shared cinnamon rolls, a baker talks to a grieving couple of loneliness and the three find a human connection as they break bread. But my students look so tired, physically and mentally, that it seems foolish to offer rewards when what they need is sustenance. So I pull out the boxes of buns, the juice and the cups, thinking only how happy they'll be to have something good to eat, a jolt of sugar to get them through the morning. Then, as I place the boxes on a desk, I realize my students are staring at me. Anna and Brian have lifted their heads, and she says, her voice bewildered, "I don't believe it." Alex chimes in, "You are the coolest teacher ever." And it seems to me that I should be giving them gold or silver or brand-new cars, something more than cinnamon buns.

I am not the coolest teacher ever. I can be curt and cranky and sometimes not so very understanding. But what I realize as I watch my students lift white iced cinnamon buns to their lips in an almost reverential way is that this is a small, good thing in precisely the way Carver meant it. This is a moment when human beings connect unexpectedly. We connect in simple kindness, and it comes on both sides.

We're finishing the buns, and Anna's head—and hand—are raised as we talk about the story. I tease her, "I guess you just needed a sugar boost, right?"

She shakes her head and speaks with a gravity I've not heard before. "I'm doing this out of respect," she says. "For you. For being nice to us. When you don't have to be."

And I understand then that we are all living in Carver's world, and though it *is* an often hard and hurtful one, we, like the baker, can make it a little sweeter, and all it takes is a small, good thing.

4 Love, Faith, and Mystery

■■■■■■■■■■■■■■■■■■■■■■■■■■■■■■■

> You simply go out and shut the door
> without thinking. And when you look back
> at what you've done
> it's too late. If this sounds
> like the story of a life, okay.
> —Raymond Carver, from "Locking
> Yourself Out, Then Trying to Get Back In"

"*That's* a poem?" Jeremy's voice is incredulous, but I could have predicted this reaction. Every year when my students read the opening lines of Carver's poem "Locking Yourself Out, Then Trying to Get Back In," their immediate response is disbelief. This doesn't sound like the poetry they're used to reading in school. Where's the rhyme? The meter? The "hidden message"? After reading a number of Carver's short stories, they've come to respect and often even love Carver as a fiction writer—but as a poet? They look at me with doubtful eyes.

What *I* know, without a doubt, is that they will ultimately like Carver's poetry for the very reasons they at first question it, and I know too that, through their reading of Carver's work, they will ultimately understand the true spirit of poetry. Carver wrote, "Every poem is an act of love, and faith" (McCaffery and Gregory 72), and any lover of poetry would agree. But adolescents aren't typically lovers of poetry, and often they see the structure and substance of poetry as enigmatic and incomprehensible—and not very interesting. Which, I tell them, is just how Raymond Carver felt.

> Rilke is quoted as saying, "Poetry is experience." That's partly it. In any event, one always recognizes the real article from the trumped-up ersatz product which is so often top-heavy with technique and intellection and struggling to "say" something. I'm tired of reading poems that are just well-made poems. (qtd. in Stull 179)

Carver's poetry offers readers something beyond the "well-made" poem. His poetry often tells a story, and it treads the same fine line between truth and imagination that one finds in his fiction. So too does it mimic Carver's fiction in its compression, its simplicity, and its precision. And always at its center is the truth of human feeling, often expressed in quite mundane terms. For these reasons, it's poetry that students can readily read and comprehend.

When students understand, on both an intellectual and an emotional level, what a poet is saying, they can respond to poetry in a meaningful way. This for me is the pleasure of teaching Raymond Carver's poetry. "Locking Yourself Out, Then Trying to Get Back In" is a poem that inspires some of the most powerful writing my students do. The poem, as its opening lines reveal, is something of an ode to regret, a feeling teenagers know all too well.

Looking Back: Writing on Regret

After reading the poem, we brainstorm situations in their lives that trigger regret. "Lying to your parents!" "Cheating on a girlfriend!" "Borrowing your father's car without permission." "Not studying for a chemistry test." Their ideas come fast and furiously, and I can almost see the stories playing out behind their eyes. So I set them to writing, to capturing in prose or poetry an experience that will make the reader feel that hot flush of regret.

Some students write fiction, taking just a bit of autobiography and transforming it into something new. Jesse, in a short story simply titled "Regret," creates a boy in a blue-collar family, close to his hardworking father who (in a sort of tribute to Carver) "seemed to always have a cigarette sewn to his lip." He describes the distance that develops between father and son as the boy becomes part of a tough group of teenagers, kids who "drank and did drugs and always seemed to brush up with the law." And he makes us feel the boy's pleasure in his new identity: "I actually felt powerful when I saw that look of helplessness in my parents' eyes; it made me feel like no one could touch me." It's only when the father dies during the boy's senior year in high school that the son realizes what he has lost in his quest for independence: "all the time I had thrown away, time which I could have spent with my father. Time we could have been fishing, talking about girls and baseball, the time I spent screwing off."

For some students, the regret piece is personal narrative, as absolute truth as memory can ever be. These pieces are wrenching, often difficult for the writer to write and also difficult for the reader to read. George describes a tragic accident, the horrible consequence of too much partying and perhaps a teenage trust in immortality. Yet, as George poignantly writes, "We weren't racing like everybody thinks; we were just boys being boys":

> Then we took that corner, my stomach jumped into the back of my throat, and my whole body got tingly. We saw his car demolished and smoking. He'd hit a parked van. "This isn't happening right now, it's not happening," was all that came out of our mouths. We didn't know what to do. The car looked

like a piece of crumpled up aluminum foil, and glass sparkled up the entire street like stars in the sky. None of us wanted to get out—we knew what the outcome would be—so all of us took one deep breath and gave one last shout to our boy.

—*George Simone*

What did it mean for George to write this piece? I can't know. The horror, the guilt, the regret that comes from watching a friend die a violent death is not something that can be expunged by putting words on a page, but perhaps it can be assuaged. I do know that he wrote this piece only months after the accident and that it was the first time he'd given voice to the experience in writing. Yet I don't believe it was only the assignment, the choice of the topic of regret, that inspired him to do so. I think it was the time he'd spent with "Ray," a man who writes lines like "Even though a wave of grief passed through me. / Even though I felt violently ashamed / of the injury I'd done back then" ("Locking Yourself Out, Then Trying to Get Back In" 74).

Carver speaks of poetry giving him "a chance to be intimate or open or vulnerable" (Schumacher 224). I believe my students sense this in his poetry, and it's one reason that I want them to read his work. Minimalist fiction often seems cold and distant. Although the situations described in minimalist stories are deeply human, the emotion is intentionally removed to give readers a feeling of the alienation common in contemporary life. In his poetry, however, Carver speaks more openly to his readers, and yet he still maintains a voice that is never maudlin but rather moving because of its frank honesty.

The Catalog Poem
One of my favorite writing assignments is modeled after Carver's poem "Fear," a list or catalog poem. In format the poem could not

be more cool and contemporary in that its structure mimics the lists that often drive our lives. Carver begins each line with the words "Fear of . . ." or "Fear that . . ." and completes each line with a different dread. He writes of thunderstorms and insomnia, of poverty and police, but intermingled with these concrete fears are those that are more haunting:

> Fear of not loving and fear of not loving enough.
> Fear that what I love will prove lethal to those I love.
> Fear of death.
> Fear of living too long.
>> —Raymond Carver, from "Fear"

The poem ends with a line that breaks the pattern and rhythm and, in a flash, establishes the essence of the poem, in this case the overriding fear of death.

Students take to this poem with enthusiasm. They see it as a confession of sorts as Carver entrusts them with his most intimate fears, and they empathize with the anxieties he inventories. I remember vividly George's face when he read the line "Fear of having to identify the body of a dead friend" ("Fear" 60). At the same time, they find it a simple structure to imitate, and so they tackle their own list poems with confidence and enthusiasm. The writing works particularly well as a group activity, with students working as a class or in small groups. Generally I first have the class brainstorm a list of emotions. We then choose six or eight of these emotions (joy, anger, guilt, pride, etc.) and write each at the top of a separate sheet of paper. These papers circulate around the room as students add their own ideas to the lists. *Confusion about algebra. Pride in being Asian. Frustration with too much to do and not enough time. Love for big furry dogs.* After the papers circulate for a while, we read the lists aloud and then decide on one emotion to use as the focus of a class poem, or I give each small group a different list and emotion to focus on. Although writing the poem seems easy at first, what students discover as they begin to formulate a draft is that word choice, phrasing, and rhythm are vitally important if the final poem is to read well and to have real meaning. They must also always consider, what is the essence of the poem? What's that final thought the reader should be left with? These challenges are integral to the writing of good poetry, whatever form a poem takes.

One class effort produced the poem "Joy," a sort of compendium of teenage pleasures.

> Joy of food
> Joy of Fridays
> Joy of being first
> Joy of snow days
> Joy of soft sheets
> Joy of sleep
> Joy of getting a job
> Joy of being paid
> Joy of buying something you want
> Joy of listening to music
> Joy of playing hackeysack
> Joy of dancing on stage
> Joy of pretty girls (and good-looking guys)
> Joy of that second your parents leave
> Joy of taking a chance
> Joy of hanging out with people who mean the most
> Joy of living one day at a time
>
> Yeah, that kind of joy
> Joy of living
> Of just being me.

After the last revision, each polished poem is written on poster paper and illustrated with drawings, photographs, and pictures. Hung on the classroom walls, the poems offer a vivid depiction of human feeling in a very readable design.

In a variation on this activity, students can work alone or in small groups on a poem that centers the emotion on a particular subject that evokes that emotion. In one class, for example, a group of students whose passion was skateboarding created this poem:

> Fear of knowing the danger
> Fear of falling
> Fear of the worst case scenario
> Fear of what the doctor says
> Fear of many months of healing
> Fear of the unstable ankle
> Fear of stepping back on your board
> Fear of doing it again
> Fear of everyone watching
> Fear of knowing the possibilities out there
> Fear of should I hold on or should I bail
> Fear of fear.

I like this poem and I suspect Carver would too. Not only does it describe an authentic life experience, but it also presents a kind of metaphor for the challenges of life and the need to overcome fear if we're to experience life fully. Like Carver's poetry, it's a testament to the strength of the human spirit even under adverse circumstances.

The list poem is so popular with my students that I also offer them "The Car," another Carver poem written in the catalog style. This poem is a lengthy list of descriptive phrases characterizing "the car," each line beginning with the words "The car . . ." The descriptions range from the concrete and clear—"The car with a cracked windshield," "The car that burned oil," "The car with wipers that wouldn't work" (151–52)—to those that are shadowy and hint at unspoken stories—"The car that hit the dog and kept going," "The car my daughter wrecked," "The car with payments that couldn't be met" (152). Students enjoy trying to "hear" what has not been said by imagining the stories that the poem intimates, and, having learned much about Carver, they can make very strong connections to his life.

Students also like to write their own poems focused on a concrete object that holds both history and meaning for them. Cars are obviously popular, as are pets, pieces of jewelry, sports gear, and favorite items of clothing, such as baseball caps, work boots, and jeans. Because their connection to these objects is often so ardent, their poems become something of a celebration of the object, a way of announcing, "This is mine and it matters." In creating the poem, students have to work hard to come up with the many details needed to vividly characterize their object and to distinguish it from others. This exercise alone is valuable in teaching students how much specific detail contributes to a piece of writing. Because they're writing in the language of poetry, they're challenged to make these descriptive details tight and terse, and this forces them to struggle with word choice. In addition, they must design a plan for their poem, a rationale for the order in which they list the lines, and I ask them, in the reflection sheets they hand in to me with their final drafts, to explain that rationale. Finally I encourage them to take the poem just a little bit further, to try to end the poem with a line or two that offers a quick burst of insight into its core. For Carver, the poem ends simply but slightly sorrowfully: "Car of my dreams. / My car" ("The Car" 152).

The Last Poems

Much of Carver's poetry has that poignant tone. His voice is that of a man who has seen and suffered and still survives. He frequently writes from the first-person point of view, and, in doing so, he seems to be revealing powerful moments in his own life, although the reader must always remember Carver's caveat about the integration of autobiography and imagination. Many of Carver's most compelling poems come from his collection *A New Path to the Waterfall* (1989), which he, in close work with Tess Gallagher, completed only weeks before his death. The poems appear in six sections and, in part, echo themes he explores in his fiction— among them the death of a child ("Lemonade"), the pain and powerlessness of childhood ("Suspenders"), and the complexities of familial relationships ("On an Old Photograph of My Son")—and, when read in conjunction with his short stories, allow students to explore connections between the genres. The poems are interspersed with passages from Chekhov, whose work had an enormous impact on Carver. Older students or those familiar with Chekhov's writing will be fascinated by the connections between the two writers' work. But my students are always most drawn to the poems in the final section, the poems that in a sense chronicle Carver's acceptance of death.

Four of these poems leave my students momentarily silent, shaken by the understated intensity. We read "What the Doctor Said," "Gravy," "Proposal," and finally "Late Fragment," and, through that series of poems, we travel the gamut of emotion from shock and despair to acceptance and joy. In these poems, Carver grapples with the reality of his illness, from the diagnosis of the lung cancer—"He said it doesn't look good / he said it looks bad in fact real bad / he said I counted thirty-two of them on one lung before / I quit counting them" ("What the Doctor Said" 113)—to the courageous and dogged decision to seize every moment of life that was left—"This / was it, so any holding back had to be stupid, had to be / insane and meager" ("Proposal" 116)—from an appreciation of what he had been given—"'I'm a lucky man. / I've had ten years longer than I or anyone / expected. Pure gravy'" ("Gravy" 118)—to an almost blessed acceptance of what is—"And did you get what / you wanted from this life, even so? / I did" ("Late Fragment" 122).

These poems have an extraordinary impact on my students. This is partly because we read them after we've become well acquainted with Carver and his fiction, so they've already taken "Ray" into their hearts. But it's also because these poems are so real, both in the situations described and in the emotions expressed, and no attempt is made to manipulate the reader's emotions. In a society where human tragedy is all too often exploited for the TV movie of the week or the bestseller of the month, Carver offers an antidote in his honesty and simplicity. Carver takes us to the heart of human experience, and although he never shies away from the pain and suffering inherent in life, he doesn't allow his reader (or himself) to wallow in the misery. Instead he reminds us time and time again, throughout all of his poetry, of the stubborn power of the human spirit, a power that need not be expressed in momentous acts and heroic deeds but rather in the most mundane activities: a handshake, a moment by a waterfall, or even a Reno wedding. Through his poetry, Carver makes us feel the curious beauty of being an imperfect person in an imperfect world, and he does so without ever resorting to melodrama or sentimentality. Instead, he simply "tells it like it is." And we know exactly what he means.

Igniting a Spark

With some exceptions, like the list poems inspired by "Fear" and "The Car" or the LISTEN to Me poems prompted by "To My Daughter" (see Chapter 1), Carver's poetry doesn't lend itself to strict modeling. It's not the structure (or lack of structure!) in Carver's work that I encourage my students to emulate. Rather it's the "temper" of his poems: "In poetry, my own or someone else's, I like narrative. A poem doesn't have to tell a story with a beginning, middle and end, but for me it has to keep moving, it has to step lively, it has to spark" ("On 'Bobber' and Other Poems" 191). I want my students to write poetry that "sparks," and I tell them that that means they have to take risks—with language, with form, and especially with feeling. Too often students, convinced that poetry ought to rhyme, produce poems that say very little. In their attempt to achieve rhyme, they sacrifice all meaning. What English teacher hasn't faced a poem of the ilk that reads, "When I was a kid, I loved to run / I played in my yard under the hot sun"? Of course, the budding poet doesn't *really* want to write about the hot sun, but the lure of the rhyme is too great to resist, and so it's likely that the poem will continue in its singsong manner until the writer has used up all the rhyming words such as *done* and *none* and *fun* and in the end said absolutely nothing that matters.

But maybe there *is* a story of childhood there, a story that isn't all sunlight and games. Maybe there's a story like the one Carver tells in his poem "Suspenders," the tale of a little boy who plays a thoughtless trick on his father, offering him a glass of dishwater in place of the fresh water intended to ease his hangover. Then, when the house erupts in anger, "[I] went over to the sink and dipped a glass / into the soapy water and drank off two glasses just / to show them. I love Dad, I said" ("Suspenders" 40).

This, my students understand, is a poem that sparks. It's a poem in which substance takes precedence over structure, where *what* the poet has to say matters more than *how* he says it, but where ultimately the content and the composition merge perfectly to create a poem in which the whole is more than its parts. This is when my students can begin to understand the mystery of poetry. A good poem, I tell them, says more than it appears to say. It's not simply that there's a hidden message the reader needs to ferret out, nor is it that the meaning is necessarily masked in metaphor. A good poem conveys something to its reader that may not be strictly conscious. A good poem hits the reader more in the heart than in the head, and its meaning lingers after the final line is read.

What my students realize the more they read Carver's writing is that *all* his work is poetry. That's perhaps why it's so powerful and why it stays with them while the work of other writers seems to fade from their memory. Carver himself speaks of the close connection between a short story and a poem: "I do think there is a stronger relationship between a story and a poem than there is between a story and novel. Economy and preciseness, meaningful detail, along with a sense of mystery, of something happening just under the surface of things" (Boddy 198). *Economy, preciseness, meaningful detail,* and that elusive sense of *mystery*—clearly those are the components of good poetry, and so too are they the components of Carver's fiction. When students see this connection between the story and the poem, and when they recognize the elements essential in each, suddenly poetry is demystified for them. It's no longer an esoteric and arcane literary form, what Carver, in commenting despairingly on the status of contemporary poetry, described as "like something you see in a museum"

(Stull 180). Instead, poetry becomes simply another means of human expression and one students can take pleasure in reading and writing.

Further Resources

■ The poetry of William Carlos Williams had a strong influence on Carver, and teachers may want to explore that connection with students. Of particular interest is Carver's "Poem for Hemingway and W. C. Williams" in *Fires—Essays, Poems, Stories* (1989).

5 Two Voices, Two Views

In an often quoted line from his poem "Epilogue," Robert Lowell remarked, "Yet why not say what happened?" Critics frequently connect this line to the maxim of minimalism: Tell it like it is. To say what happened, what *really* happened, is essential to minimalist fiction and certainly to Carver's work. Though his fiction blends "a little autobiography and a lot of imagination" (Simpson and Buzbee 41), it strives to paint a realistic picture of a corner of our contemporary world. But the question is, through whose eyes is that picture seen? And how does truth depend on perspective?

Carver's "Cathedral"

Carver is perhaps best known for his story "Cathedral," first published in *Atlantic Monthly* in 1981. It's one of his finest stories and one that shows evidence of a more expansive style, including something rare in Carver stories, a relatively happy ending. In this story of a man, his wife, and a visitor to their home—Robert, a blind man, who is a longtime friend of the wife—we're given detail and description of the characters and of the evening they share. We know quite a bit about the background of the wife and of Robert. The husband, the narrator of the story, remains rather shadowy except in our awareness of his discomfort in sharing an evening with a blind man—and one he seems jealous of. Most of the story resonates with a kind of cheerless mood that students come to expect of Carver's fiction. The characters, representatives of a blue-collar culture, eat cube steak and strawberry pie, drink Scotch, and make small talk. The couple's life appears narrow and diminished, and yet the narrator seems deeply distrustful of anything that might intrude to upset his constricted life. Despite this, we feel sympathy and even empathy for these characters because, as drawn by Carver, they're deeply human.

And that's the truth: they *are* deeply human, because they grew out of a real situation. The story is based on a visit paid to Tess Gallagher and Carver by Jerry Carriveau, a friend of Gallagher's, a blind man she had worked with in 1970 on a project for the division of Research and Development of the Seattle Police Department (Bassi and Pezzopane 6). Ten years later, after the death of his wife, Carriveau, like the fictional Robert, came east to visit family and friends.

The occasion was fodder for Carver's fiction, but, making the situation even more interesting, it was also fodder for Gallagher's work. In 1983, two years after "Cathedral" first appeared, Gallagher published "The Harvest" in the *Ontario Review*. This story presents a different fictionalized version of that visit. Dissatisfied with the story even after publication, Gallagher rewrote and republished it. Now called "Rain Flooding Your Campfire," it appeared first in 1996 in the *Sycamore Review* and then in her 1997 collection *At the Owl Woman Saloon*. Carver and Gallagher's two stories have since been published together in *Cattedrali/Cathedrals* edited by Gianluca Bassi and Barbara Pezzopane, an Italian publication that presents both stories in English and in Italian and includes "A Conversation with Tess Gallagher" as well as an album of photographs of Carver and Gallagher.

This is the background I give my students when we begin reading "Cathedral." They know it was inspired by an actual event, and they see two photographs of Carriveau included in *Carver Country*. But this knowledge doesn't really affect their reading of the story. Within the first few lines, they're plunged into a fictional situation that Carver has created.

(Here let me offer one caution to teachers. There's a scene in "Cathedral" in which the characters smoke marijuana. The inclusion of this activity is not gratuitous; it's truthful to the rendering of the characters, and, more important, it provides a credible reason for the fact that the husband relaxes in the company of the blind man, which allows for the very powerful ending. As always, however, teachers need to be sensitive to school and community standards in deciding if a story is appropriate for their students.)

My students are drawn to all three characters in "Cathedral." Though they berate the husband for his prejudice and small-mindedness, they nevertheless understand why he feels as he does. They see that the wife is caught in a difficult position, torn by loyalty to both her husband and her dear friend. And they sympathize with Robert, particularly with his disability and the recent loss of his wife, while they applaud the verve with which he attacks life: "'I'm always learning something. Learning never ends. It won't hurt me to learn something tonight. I got ears'" ("Cathedral" 38).

That attitude leads to the climax of the story. As the night winds down and the wife drifts off to sleep, Robert and the husband are left to their own devices. With the limitations of late-night TV, they settle on watching a show on the Middle Ages. Together they travel through western Europe visiting the great cathedrals until suddenly the husband, in a rare moment of aware-ness, says, "'Do you have any idea what a cathedral is? What they look like, that is? . . . If somebody says cathedral to you, do you have any notion what they're talking about?'" (40).

And so he finds himself called upon to describe a cathedral to Robert. The task is daunting, especially for a man like the nar-rator whose own experience and knowledge are limited and who's suffering the effects of a long day, a late night, and a lot of intoxi-cants. When he seems to give up in defeat ("'But I can't tell you what a cathedral looks like. It just isn't in me to do it.'" [44]), Robert comes up with an idea. He sends the husband for paper and pen. Robert then clasps his hand over the husband's hand and directs him to draw a cathedral.

In a wild and brilliant moment, the two "draw together," cap-turing more than spires and buttresses in their collaboration. When the wife sleepily opens her eyes to ask what's going on, she's al-most ignored, so close is the bond between Robert and her hus-band. Robert then instructs the husband to close his own eyes, and the two continue to draw. When Robert finally says, "'Take a look'" (48), the husband does not. He remains with his eyes shut, living the moment: "My eyes were still closed. I was in my house. I knew that. But I didn't feel like I was inside anything" (50).

In that final scene, one that leaves my students a little puzzled but curiously elated, we see a feature for which Carver's later fic-tion is known. This is the epiphany, a sudden moment of realiza-tion, what I always describe to students as that cartoon lightbulb beaming over a character's head. In many of Carver's later stories, such as "Cathedral" and "A Small, Good Thing," the central char-acter experiences an unexpected insight that changes him in a positive way. It's the closest, I tell my students, that Carver comes to a happy ending.

So we discuss this conclusion. We talk about how—and why—the husband has changed, and we debate whether the change is a permanent one, or one that will wear off with the alcohol and drugs that may have encouraged it. We appreciate the double meaning involved in the idea of "drawing together." We talk about the irony of the "blind leading the blind," and we consider what it really means to be able to "see." And when we've exhausted this discussion, I ask my students this: "So why cathedrals?"—and then the real conversation begins.

Up to this point, students typically haven't considered the use of cathedrals as the central image of the story to be significant. There's usually one student who says, "Late-night TV always has crazy stuff." But, I insist, television has other "crazy stuff," so what would make Carver choose a cathedral as his focus? Once we've acknowledged that a cathedral is something out of most people's ordinary experience and that it is intricate and difficult to describe, we can get to deeper, and what I believe are more meaningful, ideas. As Robert himself knows, cathedrals took generations to build: "'The men who began their life's work on them, they never lived to see the completion of their work. In that wise, bub, they're no different from the rest of us, right?'" (40). The husband emphasizes the cathedrals' height—"'They reach way up. Up and up. Toward the sky'" (42)—and we discuss the reasons for this, specifically man's desire to get closer to God. As we emphasize the grandeur of a cathedral, of a magnificence that seems to rise above the range of man, students begin to realize that Carver, with this image of cathedrals, is giving us a symbol of reaching beyond oneself. It is a spiritual symbol, though not a strictly religious one. Instead it represents a human being's ability to surpass his or her limitations, be they physical disabilities, class constraints, or, what perhaps limits us most of all, fears and prejudices. In that moving ending, when the narrator acknowledges that he doesn't feel like he was "inside anything" (50), we see that he has transcended not only the walls of his small house and blue-collar life, but also, and of much greater importance, he has moved beyond his preconceptions and his prejudices to fully connect, even if only temporarily, with another human being, a very different human being, in both the literal and figurative joining of hands.

My students may laugh at the husband's bullheadedness and may snicker as the characters light up a joint, but they never fail to be sincerely moved by the ending of this story. In "Cathedral," Carver does what he does best—he makes us appreciate both the fragility and the strength of our humanity.

Rodin's *La Cathedrale*

There's another intriguing connection to be made with "Cathedral," and it's one that I can't completely explain to my students. The French sculptor Auguste Rodin (1840–1917), known primarily for his works *The Thinker* and *The Kiss*, also created a sculpture called *La Cathedrale* (1908). Originally carved in stone, this piece shows two hands joined. The hands are both right hands, so the sculpture represents a coming together of two individuals. Yet the hands are not tightly clasped. Instead, they form a sort of arch, reminiscent of a Gothic arch, with space in between the palms and fingers. It's a beautiful and fluid piece, one that, even at first glance, expresses a sense of harmony. A photograph of the sculpture can work as a prereading discussion starter to spark interest in the story, or as a way to continue the discussion of the story after reading and to help make meaning of the cathedral as symbol.

My students are as fascinated as I am by the possible connections between Rodin's sculpture and the story, and they beg to know if Carver was inspired by *La Cathedrale*. Whether this piece had any direct influence on Carver's story, I don't know. I've found no research to indicate that it did. So for me, as I explain to my students, it's simply an example of how certain images have an inherent and intrinsic meaning for human beings. Perhaps, I tell them, some ideas *do* join us all.

Then, just as we are basking a bit in the mystical power of connections, I remind students that Gallagher had her own story to tell. It's a story inspired by the same events and begun at the same time that Carver began "Cathedral," but it's one that takes a very different view.

Gallagher's Mr. G.

In "A Conversation with Tess Gallagher" in *Cattedrali/Cathedrals*, Gallagher describes the "friendly competition" that existed between herself and Carver because of the story. She writes that "it was more than a little daunting to come to the trampled field . . . and think how to go forward. I couldn't ignore that he had already written his story" (Bassi and Pezzopane 92). She tackles this problem in the opening line of her story "Rain Flooding Your Campfire": "Mr. G.'s story, the patched-up version I'm about to set straight, starts with a blind man arriving at my house" ("Rain Flooding Your Campfire" 54). Students need only read that one line to get a sense of the tone of the story and to realize that with the cleverly named Mr. G., short for Mr. Gallivan, Gallagher is playing with the issue of power. As she explains,

> I needed to both acknowledge the existence of Ray's story as a relative of my story and also to join the stories through some

> device. Making my narrator slightly argumentative helped form
> the voice and it also worked to address the whole notion of
> two different stories being told from contending points of view.
> I gave him the double name which played off my own, yes—
> for the fun of it. It was also a play off the phrase—to gallivant
> . . . meaning to attend indiscretely [sic] upon members of the
> opposite sex. (Bassi and Pezzopane 94)

Mr. G. is not the narrator's husband (the role of her live-in partner belongs to a character named Ernest, who students quickly
determine is a play on Hemingway), but rather the narrator's co-
worker at a gas company. Mr. G., in another bit of Gallagher's
gentle mockery, is also a would-be writer, but "[n]othing he writes
gets published" ("Rain Flooding Your Campfire" 56).

In the story, the blind man, here named Norman, again pays
the narrator a visit but unexpectedly arrives a day early, and so
he's taken to a small dinner party at Mr. G.'s house. The dinners
in the two stories are quite alike in temper, with most attention
paid to food and drink, but after dinner the story takes a different
turn when Norman, Mr. G., Ernest, and the narrator return to
her house to watch a television show on missiles. There's a brief
scene in which Ernest, Norman, and Mr. G. together try to cut
out the shape of a missile to allow Norman to "feel" it, but the
incident seems somewhat insignificant, and the story doesn't end
there. Instead, the narrator and Ernest go off to bed, leaving Mr.
G. and Norman alone. From the bedroom window, the narrator
sees the two men in the yard as Mr. G. "points out" stars to Norman,
stars that not even the sighted Gallivan can actually see because
the night is cloudy. Later, the narrator awakens from a troubled
sleep, fearful that Mr. G. has gone, leaving Norman by himself
outside. That's precisely what's happened, and so she goes out to
a now starry night and leads Norman in: "as if the entire world

were watching and not watching, I guided our beautiful dark heads through a maze of stars, into my sleeping house" (86).

"Rain Flooding Your Campfire" is not an easy story for my students to make sense of. Typically, then, we approach it through a webbing exercise that allows us to explore what Gallagher is saying, particularly in relation to Carver's "Cathedral." We fill the chalkboard with "Things to Think About," among them the significance of the viewpoint; the meaning of the title (the phrase refers to a saying the narrator and Norman shared when things did not go well); the connections between missiles, stars, and cathedrals; the "jabs" toward Carver and his version of the story; the instances of sharply different and sharply similar scenes; and the idea of the "'marble-cake' effect" (58). After we've generated some of these basic topics for discussion, the class breaks into small groups, with each exploring a different topic in depth. Finally each group shares with the entire class its ideas and conclusions.

I like best to talk about the "'marble-cake' effect" ("Rain Flooding Your Campfire" 58). The narrator of Gallagher's story refers to this when speaking of Mr. G.'s writing ability:

> If Mr. G. were an out-and-out liar I would have more respect for his storytelling. As it is, he can't imagine anything unless he gouges himself with the truth, and that makes it hard for those who know what really happened. The result is the "marble-cake" effect. (58)

It's an appreciation for this blend of truth and fiction, the vanilla and the chocolate, that I want students to take from our discussion of these two stories. I want them to understand how truth—especially in the form of personal experience—*does* influence fiction, and how "truth" is more malleable than they might ever have imagined. An old friend arrives for a visit, and those involved experience the event from two very different perspectives. Both decide to translate it into fiction—and two totally different stories are created. Though the stories share a basic premise and plot, there are major differences in perspective and purpose. There is, for example, a keen difference between the use of a missile and a cathedral as a central symbol; as Gallagher explains, her choice was very much intended and dependent on her view of the world. Her focus was on the political "since we were very concerned at that time about the 'star wars' initiative" (Bassi and Pezzopane 104). She says too that "choosing a female narrator for my own story was a political choice, actually" (106). For Carver, politics were not an issue. "Cathedral" seems rather to be a declaration, in certain respects, of a new personal and professional direction he was taking.

Students can debate which story is more interesting, more effective, or more appealing, but I want them to go deeper to see what matters to each writer and to explore how experience alters one's view of the world. I always remind them too that were Robert/Norman to tell *his* version of the story, we'd see an entirely different angle. This poses a challenging writing assignment for students—to rewrite a scene from either story from the point of view of the blind man.

Fact to Fiction

Student writers can branch off from their discussion of the similarities and differences between "Cathedral" and "Rain Flooding Your Campfire" to tackle a variety of writing assignments in which viewpoint is the essence of the piece. For all of these assignments, I always tell students to "play with" the truth, and I encourage them to invent material in order to make a stronger story. Possible topics for such pieces include:

■ Write about an argument between you and a parent. Tell the story twice, once from your viewpoint and once from the viewpoint of your mother or father.

■ Re-create a moment when you felt misunderstood. Retell the story in the voice of one of the people who seemed to misunderstand you.

■ Describe a small but significant moment in your life. Then tell it from the point of view of someone of the opposite gender.

■ Share an experience you've had recently. Then imagine yourself twenty years in the future and recount the story.

Each of these exercises requires the writer to rethink perspective and to recognize how each writer brings to every story he or she tells a personal vision and a personal truth. From this, students move to a bigger project—a Fact to Fiction design that can be shaped and adapted to fit almost any class and curriculum.

Student writers are often asked to do memoir, to write personal essays that capture an experience or moment in their lives. This project begins with that assignment. Each student completes a personal narrative, an essay that relates, as truthfully as memory will allow, a meaningful moment in his or her life. Teachers can use a variety of prompts and activities to promote good memoir writing. Some possibilities include prewriting exercises such as:

■ Recall one particular family dinner. List every detail you can remember about it.

■ Describe a powerful smell, pleasant or unpleasant, from your childhood.

- Who were the three most important people in your life in your elementary school years? Describe each.

- Freewrite about something in your life that still haunts you.

- What were you very good at as a child? What could you never do well? Freewrite on each.

- What nicknames have you had in your life? Who gave each to you—and why?

- Describe a moment in your life that you would want to relive. Describe a moment you would never want to relive.

- Describe a time you laughed so hard that it hurt.

What I stress to students as they begin to work on their first drafts is that they need to choose an experience that is small enough for them to do justice to it in a short paper. That doesn't mean the incident is minor in terms of its significance in the writer's life; rather, it means that it happened in a fairly narrow space of time, that it's truly *an* incident, not a cumulative series of events over time.

This memoir piece is done as a distinct and separate assignment, and the teacher can allow however much time she or he feels is necessary for prewriting, writing, response, and revision. When I do this project, I grade this memoir as a complete assignment—and then I allow it to take on a brand-new life.

The second part of this project works especially well if it can be conducted between two classes, such as two sections of sophomore English or two sections of a creative writing course. I've also done this in partnership with another teacher, with our two different classes exchanging work and collaborating on the activity.

The first step in the collaboration demands that the writer of the memoir reduce his or her narrative to a one-line plot description. In doing so, students often discover that many of their plots sound similar despite the fact that the essays themselves are quite different. So we read lines like "teenage girl forced to move because of her parents' divorce" and "young boy hates mother's fiancé." Other sample plot lines include "four-year-old sent to hospital for surgery," "young girls exploring woodland find something unusual," and "neighborhood youth becomes a hero." These brief lines have the ring of a TV show preview, and they make my students laugh because they frequently sound so clichéd. This gives me ample opportunity to discuss the idea that there *are* only so many plots in literature and that it's not the writer's job to invent an entirely new plot, but rather to give unique voice and perspective to a story that has likely been told, in some form, before.

Each student writes the plot line on a strip of paper, and we send these papers to the other class. (This can be done within the same class, with students swapping plot lines among themselves; however, it's more challenging for students if they don't have easy access to the original writer and her or his memoir.)

Faced with an envelope full of plot lines, each student randomly chooses one to become the inspiration for the fictional story he or she will write. As the sample plot lines listed previously indicate, the writer has very little to go on, generally just a basic character(s) and only the briefest description of action. But it's enough. Students take to this activity with enthusiasm and imagination. Because they're not floundering to come up with an original idea, some of that "What can I write about?" paralysis is alleviated, and students take pleasure in the permission they've been given to play with someone else's life and to distort the truth.

Fashioning Fiction

At this stage, teachers can allow students to jump feet first into story writing, or they can steer students with activities designed to teach them how to create characters, write effective dialogue, describe settings, and handle other aspects of fiction writing. The choice depends on the focus and content of the course and on the time the teacher can give to the project.

If I want my students to work on creating vivid characters, then we take the time to closely examine sample character sketches and/or the lines of character description in the literature we're studying. As students attempt to create believable characters, they need to think about what reveals character, and my favorite strategy is to suggest to them a scenario in which they find themselves on a blind date. I ask them to tell me what they would judge their new acquaintance on, and the list we put together on the board is always lengthy. At first they emphasize the importance of the physical—looks, dress, mannerisms, and gestures—but then they move to other, more substantial things. They want to know their date's interests, talents, and tastes (with music being of primary importance!). They're interested in family background, social class, and ethnic and religious connections. They want to know if this potential boyfriend or girlfriend has a sense of humor, is extroverted or introverted, takes risks, speaks his or her mind, and so on. When we survey the entire list we've concocted, then I can point out that these are the same characteristics and attributes that define a fictional character, and that it's essential that the writer know her or his characters inside and out in order to bring them to life on a page. Therefore, for the main characters in their stories, students must craft a character sheet that lists almost everything one would want to know about the character, whether or not that information ever appears in the story.

Sometimes we spend time experimenting with dialogue, and we talk about the importance of diction, pace, tone, and tags. We read samples of good strong dialogue, not only listening to the words but also noting the arrangement and positioning of the words in order to create a certain voice and effect. Typically I ask students to write a monologue, connected to the central conflict in their story, in the voice of the main character. They share these with one another in response groups, with their main task being to determine how real the voice sounds.

Since a story needs to be grounded and has to happen somewhere, we often work on short pieces of description that capture a setting. I always remind students that the setting is the backdrop, like the scenery in a play, and so it shouldn't overwhelm the characters or the action. Nevertheless, it's an essential ingredient in a short story and one that students tend to ignore. So I give them prompts designed to produce vivid and specific descriptive details, and they respond in quick one- or two-line phrases. Prompts include:

- Give one visual detail to describe the place where your story happens.

- Describe a sound you would hear in this place.

- Describe a smell associated with this place.

- Describe some part of the scene, incorporating a very specific color.

- Explain what emotion or mood this place evokes.

- Describe a positive and a negative aspect of this place.

- Invent a comparison (using *like* or *as*) between this place and another.

Once students have accumulated a number of good details, they can then work on organizing the material and integrating it into the actual story.

All of these activities and assignments can be adapted to fit a teacher's schedule and goals. No matter what work precedes it, the ultimate objective is for each student to write a complete story, employing the elements of fiction, that is based on the character and plot inspired by another student's memoir. Although this is a challenging task, it's one that students enjoy, and they love sharing the final product with the original memoir writer. In fact, I think it's the anticipation of this form of publishing that motivates students to work hard on their pieces.

When all stories are complete and polished in final draft form, we take a class period to swap them back again with the memoir writer. At this point, students read both pieces together. In doing so, they truly share each other's work in a way that joins them as something close to collaborators. I ask each memoirist to then write a short letter to the story writer, offering a reaction to the story. We end the project with a discussion of the creative process and what it means to "give birth" to a story. Through their work, students discover that fiction flows from experience and from the unique perspective that each writer brings to his or her work. It is from this vision and this view that voice grows and art is born.

Further Resources

■ The Rodin Museum hosts an official Rodin Web site at www.musee-rodin.fr/welcome.htm. A variety of sculpture galleries (use www.google.com to search "Rodin Cathedrale"—without the quotation marks) offer excellent images of *La Cathedrale*.

Interlude: It Was Tess

"I saw her," Brian says, as he rushes in with the bell and a crowd of classmates. I'm shuffling through papers on my desk, thinking that it won't be easy to get a class discussion going on Carver's story "One More Thing" at 7:50 on a Monday morning.

I look up. He's watching my face eagerly, waiting for me to say something.

"You saw her?" I say, my brain struggling to think who this *her* is. I give up. "Her who?"

"Tess!" Brian says, and I detect an unspoken *Who else could it be?* "Tess Gallagher. I saw her yesterday. Where I work."

OK, I remind myself, it *is* Monday morning; maybe my brain's working just a bit slowly. But something tells me that it's unlikely Tess Gallagher wandered into the little coffee shop where I know Brian works. It's a long haul from Port Angeles, Washington, to the middle of Massachusetts, no matter how good the coffee may be. But maybe I've missed something.

"You saw Tess Gallagher? At the coffee shop?" I repeat. "Yesterday?"

By now the rest of the class is listening, this conversation more intriguing than the morning announcements rattling over the PA. I wonder for a minute if this is some class joke they're playing on me, but Brain looks so earnest and his classmates look so puzzled that a prank seems doubtful.

"All right," I say. "Start from the beginning. Tell us what happened."

And so he does. He launches into a story of Sunday morning, the usual customers and the usual orders. Scrambled eggs and sausage, blueberry muffins and coffee, a little backup at the grill, and then, "Then," he says, "she walked in.

"She was alone," Brian tells us, and he begins to describe her, the long dark hair, the half-smile, the "poet look." "You know," he says. I do; we all do. Tess Gallagher is an attractive and distinctive-looking woman. She doesn't resemble the soccer moms and neighborhood women who patronize the coffee shop. In the photographs we've seen, she has an artistic flair and presence that speaks "poet."

"But Brian," I say, "it really doesn't make sense. What would she be doing here? All by herself? All the way across the country? I haven't heard of her speaking anywhere." Now maybe even I'm trying to find a logical reason for her appearance. Maybe I want it to be Tess.

"It was Tess," he insists, obviously more willing than I to believe in semimiracles.

"Did you talk to her?" someone calls from the back of the room, and I'm listening for a note of ridicule, wanting suddenly to protect Brian from those who doubt him. But I don't hear it.

"Did you ask her about Ray?" says Angie.

"Did you tell her we've been reading her stuff?"

As the questions whirl about me, the moment feels surreal. Here we sit in a high school classroom engaged in conversation about what it was like to meet Tess Gallagher, while it seems that all of us, except maybe Brian, know it didn't happen—and yet we wish it had. We know it wasn't Tess, but we want it to be.

I'm certain that Brain isn't inventing this. He doesn't have any far-fetched stories of sitting down to chat with Gallagher, of hearing her tell tales of Carver, or of listening to her read a poem. He tells us simply that he served her coffee—"Black," he says—and a corn muffin, that she sat alone, that she read the *Globe*, and that she left. "But it was Tess," he says, and I know he believes. And the rest of us nod.

I don't have any trouble talking about "One More Thing" that morning, and in fact I wonder why I worried that I would. Once again I've been reminded of how powerfully Carver enters my students' lives. L.D. hurling a jar of pickles, Tess Gallagher ordering a corn muffin—it's all real to them and it matters because Carver makes it matter. Carver has given them a world in which people do mundane things, and yet these things have meaning beyond anything we could imagine.

The bell rings. The students troop out. Brian is the last to leave. He stops by my desk. "One more thing," he says, and in my head I'm smiling at his unwitting choice of words. For the first time he's a little shy. Slowly he reaches into his pocket and pulls out a thin white napkin. He unfolds it, revealing a faint brown coffee stain. "I kept it," he says simply, and then the napkin disappears inside his jeans and he is gone.

6 Taking a Critical Stance

"'America has just lost the writer it could least afford to lose'" (Max 36). These words, spoken at a service for Raymond Carver, summarize for me the stature and status of the man and his work at the time of his death. In his memorial for Carver, Robert Gottlieb, then editor of the *New Yorker*, presented a concise (dare I say minimalist?) statement of Raymond Carver's position in the American literary world. Carver's death ended too early a literary career that began too late. His first story was published in 1967 and his first major-press book in 1976. In 1988 he was dead. Yet in barely twenty years he produced a body of work that changed the direction of American fiction and gave voice to what had been a silent segment of American society.

When we begin any critical discussion of Carver's writing, I always remind my students of the need to acknowledge these contributions Carver made to American literature. I hope too that they will appreciate the significance of the loss of a writer at his prime. Beyond that I listen to them, wanting to hear their honest opinions of and reactions toward his work, because I think that's what Carver would have wanted—to hear his readers "tell it like it is."

Though I frequently share short excerpts and quotes from essays by critics and reviewers on writers we study, I'm reluctant to have my students examine critical commentary too closely before they've formed their own opinions on a writer's work. I want my students to know that beauty in writing, as in all art, is subjective and truly in the eyes of the beholder. Each reader has a right—and even a responsibility—to form her or his own opinions, based on that reader's reading and understanding of a piece of literature, and to be able to support those opinions with solid reasons. Students are all too willing to believe that a piece of writing is good (or bad) simply because someone older, wiser, and maybe more educated has said so, and that it's the credibility and credentials of the critic rather than the content of the piece that matter. So in my classroom, "taking a critical stance" first means standing on your own feet, making up your own mind, and defending your own opinions.

Writing a Review

Though students are sometimes initially hesitant to offer a review, I remind them that in fact they do it all the time. How many days do I come into class to hear the conversation swirling around the newest movie or CD, the latest television show, or even the food served that day in the cafeteria? The kinds of comments students make on the performance of a particular actor, the style of a certain band, or even the taste of chicken nuggets are all similar to those that critics offer when they compose a review of a writer's novel or story collection.

With that encouragement and after we've read a number of Carver's stories and poems, I set my students to writing a review of his work. I do offer them sample reviews—movie reviews taken from the newspaper, restaurant reviews clipped from magazines, and book reviews torn from the *New York Times Book Review* and other publications—to help them see how style and voice give flavor to the factual content. Carver himself wrote book reviews, some of which are collected in *No Heroics, Please* and later re-printed in *Call If You Need Me*, and these make interesting reading for students, allowing them to see how Carver's distinctive fictional voice infuses his nonfiction as well. Students can often contribute reviews from the music, game, and sports magazines they read, and these reviews, frequently of material with which teenagers are very familiar, can be especially helpful as models. As we peruse these sample reviews, we come up with some basic guidelines for their own writing.

- The review should be relatively short, with opinions delivered in a clear, concise manner.

- The factual material must be correct. Check all facts pertaining to the writer and the literature.

- The review should be firm and assertive, not wishy-washy. A reviewer must have a strong opinion.

- The reviewer is entitled to whatever opinion he or she has of the work, be it positive or negative, but it must be substantiated with details and examples.

- The reviewer should establish a voice, tone, and personal style that make the review interesting.

Finally, my students, perhaps having had more than one movie spoiled by a too-comprehensive review, usually contribute one last suggestion: "Don't give the story away! Don't tell the ending!"—and sometimes one less-than-enthusiastic Carver reviewer will add sardonically, "He doesn't write endings anyway!"

The reviews my students write may never be confused with those in the *New Yorker,* the *Atlantic* or the *New York Times Book Review*, but they're honest and heartfelt and often quite clever.

Chris calls his "Carving Your Way into Literary Renown" and extols the virtues of minimalism.

> [D]espite the ability that he [Carver] has to keep us enthralled, to keep our eyes glued to every word, Carver's early stories are incredibly minimalist, stripping away all extraneous details such as names, faces, and description, leaving us solely with what happened and a brief, if present at all, vestige of mood. However, does he really need any padding? Carver is able to pack so much into a small vessel that, at the end of a two page story, you feel as though you've just finished *Anna Karenina*. If it were Carver instead of Tolstoy, we would only have been given a brief description of Anna as she threw herself under the train— yet we would feel for her just as much without the five hundred odd pages behind it.
>
> —*Christopher Dino*

Casey, in his "Everybody Loves Raymond . . . Carver!" review, opens with a frank admission of his initial lack of interest in reading Carver: "As I sat on my bed, I pulled the story out of my backpack and glanced at the clock. It was after midnight and I didn't want to read at all. The story was titled 'Little Things' and it was only a couple of pages, so I figured I could pull through." He ends up feeling positive about "Little Things"—"This story kept me very entertained and was a valid reason to stay up past midnight on a school night"—and he continues the review by discussing similarities with "The Bath":

> Carver is one of those writers who says what he means and means what he says. He keeps things short and to the point, not even giving the reader a chance to get bored. He seamlessly alternates between narrative and dialogue, allowing the whole story to flow together. . . . Carver ends both stories with a

hanging line, leaving the true ending up to the imagination of the reader.

—*Casey Nunez*

Matt, in his review, reminds me that *contemporary* is a relative term when he talks about the value of reading Carver to learn about 1970s culture ("This was most interesting to me because I haven't read too many books that show [this part of] modern culture and how life was then."). He then focuses on a quality of Carver's fiction that even many adult readers have been known to miss.

> Carver's short stories have so many qualities not found in most I've read, things like odd humor and random situations. The first short story I read was "The Bath." It opens normally, portraying an ordinary American family preparing for a child's birthday. All seems well until the child is struck by a car, and the boy's friend can't decide whether to finish a bag of chips or continue to school. I found this odd at first and then couldn't help but laugh at the situation. This kind of deadpan humor repeats itself throughout most of his stories.
>
> —*Matthew Merritt*

Reviewing the Reviews

When, as in this instance, students raise an idea in their reviews that professional critics also reflect on, it presents a perfect opportunity to introduce critical commentary naturally into class discussion in order to promote a deeper understanding of the literature. So, with Matt's words in mind, we can discuss David Gates's comments in his 1988 *Newsweek* review "Carver: To Make a Long Story Short."

> Believers in a grim minimalist Carver miss the fun of such comic figures as the fat restaurant customer who speaks in the royal

"we," the blind, bearded house guest who calls people "Bub," his uncomfortable host ("A beard on a blind man! Too much, I say") and the old woman who natters on like a Beckett character about wanting a clock radio. Other readers see these people only as grotesques and miss their basic decency. (70)

This sort of commentary, from both students and critics, opens the door for a lively exchange. "How funny *is* Carver?" I ask, and we are off into debate, with some students laughing out loud as they cite more examples of Carver's black humor and others not convinced that he ever intended to be funny at all.

This, I think, is one of the most effective ways to use critical commentary in the classroom—to spur classroom discussion. I like to take excerpts from reviews and present them to the class, asking students to offer their own opinions on critics' remarks and judgments. One of my favorite classroom activities gets the entire class involved in an introduction to the concept of critical commentary. I choose eight or ten lines from a variety of critical essays and reviews and write each line with its source on a separate large sheet of paper. I then post these pieces of paper around the room. Students circulate around the room, reading the quotes and responding to them in writing on the paper. Their comments may be in direct response to the quote itself, or a written comment may be a reaction to another student's response. I ask students to initial each of their comments, or, if we have colored pencils available, I ask each student to choose a specific color for his or her responses.

This activity forces all students to "have something to say" and to express their views in a concise manner. It also makes them "listen" to what other students have to say. As a follow-up to the activity, I break the class into pairs or small groups, giving each group one of the papers that's now filled with ideas and opinions. The job of each group is to sift through the material in order to come up with conclusions based on their classmates' responses to the critical commentary. The following are some lines that have generated interesting reactions among students.

> The splendid truth of Carver's stories lies in what *hasn't* happened yet. (Caldwell 244)

> One aspect of what Carver seemed to say to us—even to someone who had never been inside a lumber mill or trailer park— was that literature could be fashioned out of a strict observation of real life. (McInerney 24)

> Carver's characters know a good deal less than the author does. . . . The intelligence of the stories is communicated over their heads, so to speak, from author to reader, and it is this quality which has led more than one critic to observe a note of condescension in some of the stories. (Weber 94)

> Carver's figures are haunted by the dream of a dream, or by something even more tenuous than that. (Nesset 102)

Sometimes we read more extensive pieces of commentary, and I might then have students freewrite individual responses to share with the class in a group discussion, or I might split the class into small groups to discuss a particular piece of commentary, or I might ask pairs of students to take sides, one to prove the reviewer is "right" and the other to prove him or her "wrong." The following excerpts are taken from articles and reviews that work especially well to encourage discussion. (The complete pieces are listed in the bibliography.) The first, taken from Marilynne Robinson's lengthy 1988 review of *Where I'm Calling From* in the *New York Times Book Review*, definitely gets students talking, partly because it's not entirely positive about the Carver most have come to love.

> Raymond Carver is not an easy writer to read. His narratives are often coarse. Sometimes he seems intent on proving that insensitive people have feelings, too. And while the impulse is generous, the experience of looking at the world through the eyes of a character as crude as the narrator of "Cathedral," for example, is highly uncongenial. (41)

Russell Banks, in "Raymond Carver: Our Stephen Crane," an August 1991 review of Sam Halpert's book . . . *when we talk about Raymond Carver*, offers a provocative comment on what he sees as the importance of separating the man from his work. This observation always provokes classroom conversation about the intent of Carver's fiction:

> Carver's essential sweetness, decency, and humility, his very naturalness, used as a gloss on his stories and poems, can make it difficult to see these brilliantly conceived and executed works of art in terms of their intellectually demanding themes and their disciplined darkness. It's easier to think they're about *him*, not us, to think they're autobiography, not moral history, transcription, not art. (100)

Banks goes on to decry the limitations of the minimalist label, calling it "the brand-name fallacy. It comes from the desires and needs of the publishing industry and its flacks to create niches and schools of fiction, establishing every few years a 'new thing,' such as minimalism, K-mart fiction, or dirty realism" (100). He believes this tendency makes it too easy for readers to think they understand Carver when they have only scratched the surface.

> In the case of Carver, by naming him a minimalist or a dirty realist, we stuff him into a sack with a batch of writers whose fiction has little or nothing to do with his. . . . Thus do we remark the rural blue-collar characters, the post-modern loneliness and alienation of their lives, the flattened plain style of the prose, the absence of authorial intrusion or affect. . . . We think we have the stories down. And, consequently we miss (or perhaps *avoid* is better) the moral rigor and risk of such fine stories as Carver's "Chef's House" and "So Much Water So Close to Home." (100)

Of course, not all critics see "moral rigor and risk" in Carver's writing, and some don't call Carver's stories "fine." Although, I admit, it does pain me a bit to be the bearer of negative observations of a writer I love, I think it's important for students to see all sides and to understand that literature is not about absolutes but rather about taste and personal preference. I want them to understand too that people can hold widely different views and still discuss them in a rational and intelligent manner. I bring to them, for example, the writing of John W. Aldridge from his book *Talents and Technicians: Literary Chic and the New Assembly-Line Fiction*. This study of contemporary literature offers, as the phrase "assembly-line fiction" suggests, a less than flattering commentary on minimalist writing. I like to read to students the section that focuses on Carver, a portion of which disputes the idea that Carver used the "iceberg approach" as effectively as Hemingway. Aldridge also speaks of Carver's "poverty of imagination" (56) and writes that

> his minimalist method comes to seem not a statement of the little he deliberately chose to say out of all he might have said but rather a confession that this is all he had to say, perhaps because his characters are simply not interesting or important

enough to deserve extended development or because he was unable to take full imaginative possession of them. (52)

Some students find in this opinion a validation of their own dissatisfaction with Carver, and there's definitely value in that. I think it gives students confidence in the strength of their own opinions when their views are echoed by others, and it teaches them to trust their own beliefs. For other students, Carver lovers like me, the negative comments of critics serve only to strengthen their leanings and their loyalty and to inspire them to think more deeply about why they like Carver's writing and to then defend their views. This is when critical commentary "works" in the classroom—when it starts students thinking, and especially when it starts them thinking about the lives they live.

Vivian Gornick, in her 1990 essay "Tenderhearted Men: Lonesome, Sad and Blue" published in the *New York Times Book Review*, offers an interesting perspective on what she see as a type of "American story that is characterized by a laconic surface and a tight-lipped speaking voice. The narrator in this story has been made inarticulate by modern life. Vulnerable to his own loneliness, he is forced into hard-boiled self-protection" (1). Gornick regards the classic Hemingway male character as the predecessor of this contemporary American "hero," one whom she sees in the fiction of Carver, Richard Ford, and Andre Dubus. Her essay explores the relationships between men and women as depicted in the work of these writers, lamenting what she calls "the extraordinarily fixed nature of what goes on between characters who are men and characters who are women" (1).

In her discussion of Carver's story "Are These Actual Miles?"— a story about a couple's bankruptcy and the resulting sale of their beloved red convertible (a story that comes straight from Carver's

105

life and one that is documented in the documentary film *To Write and Keep Kind* [Walkinshaw])—Gornick writes that Carver consistently "mourns the loss of romantic possibility" (32). She mentions a number of Carver's stories, including "Little Things," that are

> saturated in a wistful longing for an ideal tender connection that never was, and never can be. . . . In short, the work is sentimental. Trapped inside that sentimentality is the struggle so many women and so many men are waging now to make sense of themselves as they actually are. The struggle has brought men-and-women-together into a new place; puzzling and painful, true, but new nonetheless. In the country of these stories not only is that place not on the map, it's as though the territory doesn't exist. (32)

Gornick's view opens up a whole new area of discussion and one that takes us first deeper into Carver's fiction and then beyond it into a conversation about male and female roles in the twenty-first century. This, I think, is how we can make literature matter to students, when we can get them to see that the best literature grapples with the human conflicts and issues that are both individual and universal. Men and women, for example, have always struggled and likely will always struggle in their relationships with each other. The feelings that pull the man and the woman—and the baby—of "Little Things" apart are the same sort of feelings that end an adolescent's parents' marriage or, on a lesser scale, strand a teenager without a prom date. If Gornick makes us coolly examine Carver's portrayal of men and women and if she makes us question the wisdom of their expectations, then perhaps we'll look more closely at our own relationships and our own expectations. Though often we talk of a good book or story as an escape from our own ordinary lives, the truth is that the best literature succeeds because, though it may give us a picture of another place and another time, it allows us see our own reflection within.

One of my favorite essays on Carver was published in the *New York Times Book Review* a year after Carver's death. Written by Jay McInerney, a fellow writer and a student of Carver, "Raymond Carver: A Still, Small Voice" offers both critical commentary and a portrait of Carver as teacher and mentor. (This essay is reprinted as "Raymond Carver, Mentor" in *Remembering Ray* [Stull and Carroll]). In his essay, McInerney writes:

> As I say, he [Carver] mumbled. . . . I now think it was a function of a deep humility and a respect for the language bordering on awe, a reflection of his sense that words should be handled very, very gingerly. As if it might almost be impossible to say what you wanted to say. As if it might be dangerous, even. . . . [Y]ou sensed a writer who loved the words of the masters who had handed the language down to him, and who was concerned that he might not be worthy to pick up the instrument. (McInerney 1, 24)

As we end our study of Carver, I read these lines to my students, and I think they hear them as another sort of memorial to him. McInerney reminds us that Carver was a man who came to writing from the outside. He was a boy with a hard-luck life who found his passion in writing and followed it. Words saved him, and so he understood that though it might be dangerous, almost impossible, to say what you had to say, you did it anyway, because words were what you had when you didn't have anything else.

Carver's words have changed many of my students' lives. For some of them, his world is immediately a familiar one. For others, more affluent and perhaps more entitled, it at first seems somewhat alien. But Carver makes all of us realize that no matter what class, what color, or what race a person is, he or she still inhabits a corner of Carver Country. No one escapes the essential alienation of contemporary life. For that reason, reading Raymond Carver is "a small, good thing in a time like this" ("A Small, Good Thing" 404). Carver reminds us that in the loneliness we share, we find a connection with one another, a bond to sweeten life like a cinnamon bun.

Chronology of Raymond Carver's Life

1938   Raymond Clevie Carver Jr. is born on May 25 in
        Clatskanie, Oregon, to Clevie Raymond Carver and
        Ella Beatrice Casey.

1941   Carver family moves to Yakima, Washington.

1956   Carver graduates from Yakima High School.

1957   Carver marries Maryann Burk. His daughter is born in
        December.

1958   Carver moves with wife and daughter to California.
        He studies part time at Chico State College. His son
        is born in October.

1959   Carver begins studying with John Gardner at Chico
        State College.

1960   Carver moves family to Eureka, California, to find
        employment. He enrolls at Humboldt State College.

1963   Carver graduates from Humboldt. He receives a
        fellowship to attend the Iowa Writers' Workshop.

1967   Carvers file for bankruptcy. Carver's father dies.
        Carver meets editor Gordon Lish, and his story "Will
        You Please Be Quiet, Please?" is published in *The Best
        American Short Stories 1967.*

1968   Carver's drinking increases.

1970   Carver is awarded a National Endowment for the
        Arts Discovery Award and begins to write full time.

1971   *Esquire* publishes "Neighbors."

1972   Carver receives a Wallace E. Stegner Fellowship at
        Stanford University.

1973   "What Is It?" is published in the O. Henry Awards'
        Prize Stories 1973. Carver teaches at the Iowa Writ-
        ers' Workshop.

1974   Carver's drinking increases and family problems
        mount. He resigns his teaching position at UC Santa
        Barbara and declares bankruptcy. His writing suffers.

1976   Carver is hospitalized repeatedly for alcohol-related
        problems. He publishes his first major-press book,
        Will You Please Be Quiet, Please?

1977   Carvers temporarily separate but reconcile. On June
        2 he stops drinking. He meets Tess Gallagher for the
        first time at a writers' conference.

1978   Carvers separate.

1979   Carver and Gallagher begin living together, traveling between Texas, Washington, Arizona, and New York as their teaching positions require.

1981   *What We Talk About When We Talk About Love* is published, with controversial editing decisions made by Gordon Lish. The *New Yorker* publishes Carver for the first time with "Chef's House."

1982   "Cathedral" appears in *The Best American Short Stories 1982*. The Carvers are legally divorced.

1983   *Fires: Essays, Poems, Stories* is published. Carver receives a Mildred and Harold Strauss Livings Award from the American Academy and Institute of Arts and Letters. *Cathedral* is published and wins a National Book Critics Circle Award nomination.

1984   *Cathedral* earns a Pulitzer Prize nomination. Carver continues to write fiction and begins to focus more on poetry. He and Gallagher live part of the year in Port Angeles, Washington, and part in Syracuse, New York.

1985   Carver's poems are published in *Poetry* magazine. His collection of poetry *Where Water Comes Together with Other Water* is published.

1986   *Ultramarine*, a poetry collection, is published.

1987   "Errand," the last story published before Carver's
            death, appears in the June 1 *New Yorker*. Carver is
            diagnosed with lung cancer and in October under-
            goes surgery.

1988   Carver's cancer reappears and he faces radiation
            treatments. His short story collection *Where I'm
            Calling From* is published. He is inducted into the
            American Academy and Institute of Arts and Letters.
            On June 17, Carver and Gallagher marry in Reno,
            Nevada. Carver works on his final book of poetry, *A
            New Path to the Waterfall*. He dies on August 2 and is
            buried in Port Angeles.

1989   *A New Path to the Waterfall* is published.

1992   *No Heroics, Please: Uncollected Writings* is published.

2001   *Call If You Need Me: The Uncollected Fiction and Other
            Prose*, an expanded edition of *No Heroics, Please*, is
            published.

Bibliography

ALDRIDGE, JOHN W. 1992. *Talents and Technicians: Literary Chic and the New Assembly-Line Fiction.* New York: Scribner's.

APPLEFIELD, DAVID. "Fiction & America: Raymond Carver." In Gentry and Stull, *Conversations with Raymond Carver,* 204–13.

BANKS, RUSSELL. 1991. "Raymond Carver: Our Stephen Crane." *Atlantic* (August): 99–103.

BASSI, GIANLUCA, AND BARBARA PEZZOPANE, EDS. 2002. *Cattedrali/Cathedrals.* Rome: Leconte Editore.

BODDY, KASIA. "A Conversation." In Gentry and Stull, *Conversations with Raymond Carver,* 197–203.

BONETTI, KAY. "Ray Carver: Keeping It Short." In Gentry and Stull, *Conversations with Raymond Carver,* 53–61.

CALDWELL, GAIL. "Raymond Carver: Darkness Dominates His Books, Not His Life." In Gentry and Stull, *Conversations with Raymond Carver,* 243–48.

CARVER, RAYMOND. 2000. *All of Us: The Collected Poems.* New York: Vintage Contemporaries.

———. "The Autopsy Room." In *All of Us: The Collected Poems,* 149–50.

———. "The Bath." In *What We Talk About When We Talk About Love,* 47–56.

———. "Bicycles, Muscles, Cigarettes." In *Where I'm Calling From,* 21–33.

———. 2001. *Call If You Need Me: The Uncollected Fiction and Other Prose.* William L. Stull, ed. New York: Vintage Contemporaries.

―――. "The Car." In *All of Us: The Collected Poems*, 151–52.

―――. 1994. *Carver Country: The World of Raymond Carver*. New York: Arcade.

―――. 1983. *Cathedral*. New York: Knopf.

―――. "Cathedral." In Bassi and Pezzopane, *Cattedrali/Cathedrals*. 11–51.

―――. "Distance." In *Where I'm Calling From*, 186–97.

―――. "Everything Stuck to Him." In *What We Talk About When We Talk About Love*, 127–35.

―――. "Fear." In *All of Us: The Collected Poems*, 60.

―――. 1989. *Fires: Essays, Poems, Stories*. New York: Vintage Contemporaries.

―――. "Fires." In *Call If You Need Me*, 93–106.

―――. "Gravy." In *A New Path to the Waterfall*, 118.

―――. "John Gardner: The Writer as Teacher." In *Call If You Need Me*, 107–14.

―――. "Late Fragment." In *A New Path to the Waterfall*, 122.

―――. "Little Things." In *Where I'm Calling From*, 152–54.

―――. "Locking Yourself Out, Then Trying to Get Back In." In *All of Us: The Collected Poems*, 73–74.

―――. "My Father's Life." In *Call If You Need Me*, 77–86.

―――. 1989. *A New Path to the Waterfall: Poems*. New York: Atlantic Monthly Press.

―――. 1992. *No Heroics, Please: Uncollected Writings*. William L. Stull, ed. New York: Vintage Books.

―――. "On 'Bobber' and Other Poems." In *Call If You Need Me*, 190–93.

―――. "One More Thing." In *Where I'm Calling From*, 147–51.

―――. "On 'Errand.'" In *Call If You Need Me*, 197–98.

————. "On Rewriting." In *No Heroics, Please*, 107–10.

————. "On Writing." In *Call If You Need Me*, 87–92.

————. "Photograph of My Father in His Twenty-Second Year." In *All of Us: The Collected Poems*, 7.

————. "Proposal." In *A New Path to the Waterfall*, 115–16.

————. "A Small, Good Thing." In *Where I'm Calling From*, 376–405.

————. "Suspenders." In *A New Path to the Waterfall*, 40–41.

————. "To My Daughter." In *All of Us: The Collected Poems*, 70–71.

————. "Wenas Ridge." In *All of Us: The Collected Poems*, 75–76.

————. "What the Doctor Said." In *A New Path to the Waterfall*, 113.

————. 1989. *What We Talk About When We Talk About Love*. New York: Vintage Books.

————. "What You Need for Painting." In *All of Us: The Collected Poems*, 142.

————. 1989. *Where I'm Calling From: New and Selected Stories*. New York: Vintage Contemporaries.

————. 1976. *Will You Please Be Quiet, Please?* New York: McGraw-Hill.

FORD, RICHARD. 1998. "Good Raymond." *New Yorker* (October 5): 70–79.

GALLAGHER, TESS. "Rain Flooding Your Campfire." In Bassi and Pezzopane, *Cattedrali/Cathedrals*, 53–87.

GATES, DAVID. 1988. "Carver: To Make a Long Story Short." Review of *Where I'm Calling From* by Raymond Carver. *Newsweek* (June 6): 70.

GENTRY, MARSHALL BRUCE, AND WILLIAM L. STULL, EDS. 1990. *Conversations with Raymond Carver*. Jackson: University Press of Mississippi.

GORNICK, VIVIAN. 1990. "Tenderhearted Men: Lonesome, Sad and Blue." *New York Times Book Review* (September 16): 1, 32–35.

HALPERT, SAM. 1995. *Raymond Carver: An Oral Biography*. Iowa City: University of Iowa Press.

HEMINGWAY, ERNEST. 1987. "Cat in the Rain." In *The Complete Short Stories of Ernest Hemingway*, 129–31. New York: Scribner's.

———. 1932. *Death in the Afternoon.* New York: Scribner's.

KELLERMAN, STEWART. 1988. "Grace Has Come into My Life." Review of *Where I'm Calling From* by Raymond Carver. *New York Times Book Review* (May 15): 40.

MARKER, SHERRY. 2003. *Edward Hopper.* North Dighton, MA: World Publications Group.

MAX, D. T. 1988. "The Carver Chronicles." *New York Times Magazine* (August 9): 34–40, 51, 56–57.

MCCAFFERY, LARRY, AND SINDA GREGORY, EDS. 1987. *Alive and Writing: Interviews with American Authors of the 1980s.* Urbana: University of Illinois Press.

MCINERNEY, JAY. 1989. "Raymond Carver: A Still, Small Voice." *New York Times Book Review* (August 6): 1, 24–25.

MOFFET, PENELOPE. "*PW* Interviews Raymond Carver." In Gentry and Stull, *Conversations with Raymond Carver*, 238–42.

NATIONAL ENDOWMENT FOR THE ARTS. 2004. *Reading at Risk: A Survey of Literary Reading in America.* Washington, DC: National Endowment for the Arts.

NESSET, KIRK. 1995. *The Stories of Raymond Carver: A Critical Study.* Athens: Ohio University Press.

POPE, ROBERT, AND LISA MCELHINNY. "Raymond Carver Speaking." In Gentry and Stull, *Conversations with Raymond Carver*, 11–23.

RIOTTA, GIANNI. "'I've Got a Book to Finish, I'm a Lucky Man.'" In Gentry and Stull, *Conversations with Raymond Carver*, 249–50.

ROBINSON, MARILYNNE. 1988. "Marriage and Other Astonishing Bonds." Review of *Where I'm Calling From* by Raymond Carver. *New York Times Book Review* (May 15): 1, 35, 40–41.

SCHUMACHER, MICHAEL. "After the Fire, into the Fire: An Interview with Raymond Carver." In Gentry and Stull, *Conversations with Raymond Carver*, 214–37.

SEXTON, DAVID. "David Sexton Talks to Raymond Carver." In Gentry and Stull, *Conversations with Raymond Carver*, 120–32.

SIMPSON, MONA, AND LEWIS BUZBEE. "Raymond Carver." In Gentry and Stull, *Conversations with Raymond Carver*, 31–52.

STEWART, ROBERT. 1993. "Reimagining Raymond Carver on Film: A Talk with Robert Altman and Tess Gallagher." *New York Times Book Review* (September 12): 3, 41–42.

STULL, WILLIAM L. "Matters of Life and Death." In Gentry and Stull, *Conversations with Raymond Carver*, 177–91.

STULL, WILLIAM L., AND MAUREEN P. CARROLL, EDS. 1993. *Remembering Ray: A Composite Biography of Raymond Carver*. Santa Barbara: Capra Press.

TROMP, HANSMAARTEN. "Any Good Writer Uses His Imagination to Convince the Reader." In Gentry and Stull, *Conversations with Raymond Carver*, 72–83.

WALKINSHAW, JEAN, PROD./DIR. 1992. *To Write and Keep Kind*. VHS. Seattle: KCTS TV.

WEBER, BRUCE. "Raymond Carver: A Chronicler of Blue-Collar Despair." In Gentry and Stull, *Conversations with Raymond Carver*, 84–97.

ZINSSER, WILLIAM. 2001. *On Writing Well: The Classic Guide to Writing Nonfiction*. New York: Quill.

Author

Susanne Rubenstein teaches English at Wachusett Regional High School in Holden, Massachusetts, and has a special interest in contemporary literature. Active in the Central Massachusetts Writing Project, she frequently presents workshops for teachers on the teaching of writing and is the author of *Go Public! Encouraging Student Writers to Publish* (1998). Her fiction and poetry have appeared in such publications as *Literal Latte*, *The MacGuffin*, and *The Worcester Review*, and her essays on teaching have been published in *The Christian Science Monitor*, *Voices from the Middle*, *School Arts*, and *Teacher Magazine* as well as a number of collections, including NCTE's *Short Stories in the Classroom*.

■ ■

This book was typeset by Electronic Imaging in Berkeley and Interstate.

The typefaces used on the cover include Trebuchet MS and Zurich Ex BT.

The book was printed on 50-lb. Williamsburg Offset paper by Versa Press, Inc.